Configuration Management Metrics

Configuration Management Metrics

Product Lifecycle and Engineering Documentation Control Measurements

Frank B. Watts, BSME, CCDM

Author of *Engineering Documentation Control Handbook*

Amsterdam • Boston • Heidelberg • London • New York • Oxford
Paris • San Diego • San Francisco • Sydney • Tokyo
William Andrew is an imprint of Elsevier

William Andrew is an imprint of Elsevier
Linacre House, Jordan Hill, Oxford OX2 8DP, UK
30 Corporate Drive, Suite 400, Burlington, MA 01803, USA

First edition 2010

British Library Cataloguing in Publication Data
Watts, Frank B.
  Configuration management metrics.
  1. Configuration management.
  I. Title
  670. 2'85-dc22

Library of Congress Control Number: 2009932551

ISBN: 978-0-08-096445-4

Printed and bound in the United States of America

09 10 11 12 11 10 9 8 7 6 5 4 3 2 1

Contents

Contents

Chapter 4 Order entry and fulfillment 85

Contents

Contents

Acknowledgements

My thanks to the universities who have sponsored my seminars and to the over 3500 folks who have attended – I learn something in each seminar.

My many customers also deserve hearty thanks since I learn something new from each of them.

Last, but not least, thanks to my wife Jane and our family for encouragement.

Readers are encouraged to contact me for any questions or corrections on this work, or to ask for a free copy of my Acronyms and Definitions standard.

Frank B. Watts, BSME, CCDM
ec3corp@rkymtnhi.com
www.ecm5tools.com
Winter Park, Colorado
April 2009

Preface

Product hardware and software documentation control, or Configuration Management (CM) if you prefer, has become a key strategy for successful manufacturing companies. Controlling the design documentation throughout its lifecycle and knowing what is in the product is very important for quickly moving a new product to the marketplace, identifying necessary changes (and unnecessary ones) and making the necessary changes as fast as possible. All this must be done with improved quality of both the documentation and the processes. CM is similarly important to efficient, high-quality and low-cost supply chain and production processes. It is also critical to maintenance, repair, retrofit, and service parts provisioning as well at the elephant in the room – liability protection.

Fast, accurate, efficient, documented, measured and well-understood Configuration Management is also critical to profitability. Properly done, CM sets the stage for innovation in both Engineering and Operations. My book (*Engineering Documentation Control Handbook – Configuration Management in Industry*) about the basics of the discipline has been very well received. Some say it has, while surpassing 10,000 copies sold, become the standard for industry.

While writing the third edition, I realized that while it contains some basic measurements for the CM/product lifecycle processes, much more needs to be said about the subject. Much more about measurements and metrics, their development, reporting and analyzing company performance in this arena is needed.

CM processes must be established and documented in order to make many meaningful measurements and reports. Process improvement is speculative without metrics to measure progress. Process documentation is required for meaningful training as well as a basis for improvement. Thus, this book is intended to fill that need.

The author's Mechanical/Industrial Engineering education and over 50 years in product manufacturing and consultation experience has evolved some basic principles about processes and their measurement:

- **Principle:** Processes are the very essence of business.
- **Principle:** Fast, accurate, efficient, documented, measured and well-understood processes are the most important key to best in class or world-class manufacturing.
- **Principle:** The first step toward solving a problem is recognition and definition of the problem – and measurement is hugely significant to both recognition and definition.
- **Principle:** Measurement, in and of itself, tends to improve performance by highlighting problems and performance, thus opening the door to improvement.
- **Principle:** Measurement, without concise reporting and high visibility, loses effectiveness.
- **Principle:** The first step toward process improvement is measurement of the process. Without measurement one cannot tell if there is, in fact, improvement.
- **Principle:** Every organization within a product manufacturing company needs to develop a few key indicators (metrics) for their portion of the operations.
- **Principle:** Every man-made process can be improved by man.

This book will be based on those principles and normally directed to the Design Engineering/Configuration Management functions. There are, of course, many measurements in operations, the supply chain, quality, service, accounting, personnel, etc. that need to be addressed in any product manufacturing company. This book will not enter those domains except as engineering's design and documentation enters them – which is considerable. Thus we will focus on the engineering, engineering documentation control and configuration management arena, across functional lines, wherever it leads us.

Light must be shed on a problem in order to produce heat (recognition of the problem), which will likely produce a solution. Thus the first step toward improvement in the CM processes is to document those processes and to measure them – to shed light on problems. Measurement doesn't necessarily point to solutions but your company may *not* know if they have a problem, and/or how serious a problem is, without measurement.

Among the myriad of potential measurements, it is easy to get lost in the abundant possibilities for reports or lost in an over-abundance of data. An effort will be made in this book to sort out the optimum data display metrics. This author considers all the metrics in this book important for the CM function to develop in the product manufacturing environment. Of course, some may not be applicable to your kind of engineering/ manufacturing. Some you will deem necessary to develop sooner, some later, some not at all. You probably will not have the resources to produce all of the metrics you might select from this work – you will thus be faced with setting priorities, selecting those most useful.

An attempt will be made to give the reader some insight as to the importance or urgency of the metrics. Methods of distributing the metrics are discussed as well as the people targeted and the method of the distribution. Since the raw data may be difficult to assess, methods of graphing or charting the data will be demonstrated. Because the data (even graphically presented) may lack perspective, benchmarking data will be included where available. Client experiences will be used without naming the clients (over 70 consulting clients at this writing).

Metrics will also tend to make the management aware of the significance of the CM function. Each reported metric will draw attention to the CM function – good or bad. The fact that a given metric may reflect poorly on the CM function should not stop us from distributing it as needed. Who knows, it might result in more resources or, as in some companies, recognition that the function should be populated with technical folks rather than purely clerical folks.

The reader will find that the approach taken by this author is, in effect, to make the CM function the Quality Assurance function for engineering design and documentation – tasks sorely needed in many product manufacturing organizations. The Quality Assurance folks generally work heavily in the manufacturing side of the business and only lightly in the design documentation side. CM should be manned and chartered to fill that gap.

The purpose of this book is to consolidate all the processes and measurements important to determine whether or not the organization has issues and something about the magnitude of those issues. It will speak only lightly to the probable solutions. Solutions are generally abundant in the *Engineering Documentation Control Handbook – Configuration Management in Industry*, referred to herein as the *EDC Handbook*.

These pages will speak to the product, including its firmware and application software. The discussions will be done using the part, assembly and product terminology. The terminology of firmware, chip, code, module and software product can be substituted in many cases.

A chapter about definitions of data, terms and acronyms is included as an invaluable reference for most CM writing, as well as a resource for writing your own standards. Plagiarize that chapter and make a separate standard for acronyms and term definitions – or better yet contact the writer for an online copy. This will allow definitions to be in one place and not duplicated in various standards or risk defining them differently in other standards.

Each chapter will outline one of the most important measures of merit – the need for written policy and procedures. Without policy, procedure, form, form instruction and associated standards, one not only has chaos but lacks foundation for improvement. The best of the best practices as to the optimum "standards" will be listed with an opportunity for the reader to "check off" those that their company has and those they don't. This will not be an exercise in ISO/QS/AS requirements but rather a make-sense approach to defining your needs for documenting the CM and related processes. Documenting your standards is not submitted as a method of encouraging you to "baffle them with BS". Rather it is expected that such standards will be a single subject in one, two or three pages and that limit will seldom be exceeded.

In these pages the Front End Loader Company product type or model numbers will be used – FEL-100 for example. This is done to give some generic but realistic flavor to the data.

Some believe that measurement and reporting on any process are not important. Those people who believe that measurement (testing) and report cards from their kids' schools are not important should read no further – unless they wish to find out why they are so significant that they need to be sent home to Mom/Dad on a timely basis and frequently, and even more frequently reviewed by the teachers and school administrators.

List of Figures

List of Tables

Chapter One

Introduction

As the engineer's saying goes, defining the problem is the first step toward solution. Understanding the processes, the volume, process time, quality and other measurements of the product lifecycle is the first step toward best-in-class design, development, configuration management, supply chain and product manufacturing.

Most product manufacturing organizations know the number of new products they release, the number of new specs and drawings they release, and the number of changes they make in any given period of time. Less than a third measure the change process time precisely according to the author's benchmarking survey of 58 product manufacturing companies. In fact, of the 31% that said they measure the change process time precisely, only four were willing to furnish their report. Does this mean that most of the 31% thought they knew their process time but didn't actually measure it? Or only measured a part of the process? Or that they had only measured the process speed at a snapshot in time? Does this mean that two-thirds or more of product manufacturing companies do not feel that speed in the change process is important? If a change is worth doing, isn't it worth doing fast?

Faster processing of new item releases, requests for engineering action, redesign and incorporation of changes and related functions is critical to profitability. If a change is required to meet specification, should we ship more products without that change? If a change will accomplish a real cost reduction should we build more products at a higher cost? If a change can logically be processed slowly, it probably shouldn't be done at all (methods of screening out unneeded or unwise changes are included). This writer would submit that any change worth doing is worth doing fast. Not at the sacrifice of quality, however – neither the quality of the change nor the quality of the product. This same analysis can be applied to the release process, request process, and every other CM and related process.

What is CM?

Let's first identify the basic "raw materials" of product manufacturing – the very essence of product manufacturing. There are three primary elements:

- Tools (machine, mold, software, etc.)
- People (and the processes they choose to follow)
- A product (embodied in design drawings, specs and code).

So why then is it a surprise for some to hear that the process control of those design documents is a critical discipline? Think about it. Without design documents, you have no product or at least no ability to produce a repeatable product. Without processes to control design documents you have chaos. Without those processes being fast, accurate, documented, measured and well understood you have serious efficiency or cost issues. Issues which take/steal time from engineers to product-innovate and manufacturing to process-innovate. Creating fast, accurate, measured, documented and well-understood processes will thus set the stage for innovation.

Why is the revelation that the processes are the very essence of business a surprise to anyone? Why do we continue to see processes in business, in government, on the internet, and in our daily lives so convoluted, complicated and non-intuitive as to be ludicrous? Without; make sense, fast, accurate and measured processes you also have a touch (or more) of insanity.

Setting the stage for innovation

An article the author wrote for APICS e-News (Feb. 2005) may help define the discipline:

> *"The basic raw materials for product manufacturing are* **tools** *(including software),* **people** *(the processes they choose) and the* **design documents***. Not withstanding this basic truth, most companies have a gap between Engineering and Manufacturing/Operations people, processes and systems with regard to design documents.*
>
> *Engineering people tend to be very analytical and cautious. Manufacturing people tend to be movers and doers. Manufacturing people say that engineers frequently 'throw it over the wall'. Engineering people say they 'can't find anyone who knows how the new product will be processed'. Manufacturing folks say*

'*Engineering is always changing the design*'. *While engineering people say* '*Manufacturing people are always changing the process*'. *Their respective processes tend to end at the water's edge, sometimes with endless meetings intended to bridge the gap between them.*

Manufacturing folks have purchased MRP/ERP systems and Supply Chain systems. Engineering purchased CAD/PDM/PLM systems. These systems seldom 'talk to each other'. Multiple Bills of Material and other major problems result.

A plethora of manufacturing and supply chain papers, articles and software programs seem to assume *the availability of the right document, at the right place, at the right time. Many folks are caught up in the 'buy a new system to solve the problem' mode. Few seem to be working on bridging the gap/tearing down the wall between engineering and operations.*

Note what Morris and Brandon wrote in Re-engineering Your Business: '*To be sure, information technology was used to support the new process, but the process redesign came first and the technology considerations second.*' *Also what Mitch Ratcliffe wrote in* Technology Review: '*A computer lets you make more mistakes faster than any invention in human history ... with the possible exceptions of handguns and tequila.*'

Yes, software solutions can help us get the right document to the right place at the right time, if (that big word) we have a process in place requiring that to happen. Much more attention needs to be focused on the design documentation/CM processes before jumping to 'the software solution'. This is true whether we are talking about manufacturing in house or via the supply chain. One needs only to analyze the root cause for 'bad parts' that end up on the dock or the manufacturing floor. Or analyze the root cause when customers receive a different configuration of a product than they wanted. Why do materials/supply chain people often have parts they don't need and/or are short of parts they do need? How many of the product changes are thought to be 'cost reductions' but aren't? This writer's experience says that the technical document processes, or lack thereof, are the root cause of a vast majority of manufacturing problems.

We need to bridge the gap between engineering and manufacturing people, processes and systems. Design the engineering documentation processes first, establish meaningful metrics, streamline the processes with legacy systems, then seek new software to facilitate that process design. Focusing on the processes first is the next great frontier for continuous improvement."

Another way of viewing the CM function is as the quality assurance function for the design and related technical documentation. CM should assure that the right person reviews the new or changed documents, at the right time, signs same, and that all document-related standards (drafting manual and CM standards) are followed. Also, CM should assure that the processes are measured and reported as appropriate to highlight problems or progress. We need to carry out these functions whether we are criticized, demonized or praised. In the long run an appreciation for the CM function will evolve.

Bridge the gap

Another way of viewing the Configuration Management organization is as the communications bridge between Design Engineering and the rest of the world (see Fig. 1.1).

Communication may be the single most important function performed by the CM organization. Communications about the process and the documentation are critical to the product lifecycle profitability. Process measurement is a basic necessity to this communication. Design the control processes, document them, communicate them and measure them.

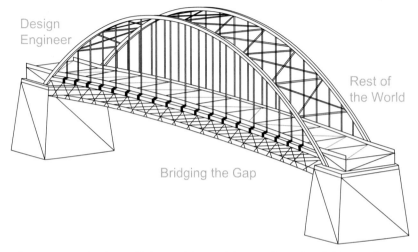

Design
Engineer

Rest of
the World

Bridging the Gap

Figure 1.1 ● CM, a bridge for communications. (Adapted from "How to Stay Flexible and Elude Fads" by DeToro and McCabe, Quality Progress, March 1987)

The measurements must be associated with all the traffic across the bridge – in both directions. Some of that traffic is of the significance of an 18-wheeler and other traffic has the significance of a walking tourist. Thus there should be a degree of significance about our measurements.

These metrics should generally be prepared by the CM manager and the CM technicians. If a key metric is prepared by another department, the CM manager should make sure it is communicated to the right people at the right time. Much of the work in preparation of the metrics discussed here (and applicable to a particular company/division) is best done by the CM function.

It is sometimes the case that no CM function exists and even if the function exists, it is not properly manned. It is often "buried" too deep in the organization. It should answer to the Chief Engineer or to the Director of Engineering Services – executive management take note. It must also be properly manned – typically with technicians.

- **Principle:** The CM function, properly chartered and manned, becomes the Quality Assurance function for the company design and related technical documentation processes.

CM Processes

In order to organize the discipline and this book, we will address the important metrics in the major CM processes and closely related processes:

- New item release
- Order entry/fulfillment
- Request for change
- Bill of material
- Change
- Change cost
- Field change.

Ancillary processes which may or may not be thought of as part of the above major processes will also be addressed, significantly – deviations, service parts, publications and field failure reporting.

Some general CM issues also need to be measured. How many products, features and options, design documents, active part numbers, files, etc. may be important items for a "knowledge database"? Such "data gathering" might not be important simply as a metric but will certainly be important to your process improvement.

Why is measurement important?

It may be that some of your people or management believe that reports are unnecessary or even a waste of time. This is the same mind-set that considers testing and school report cards unnecessary. We can intuitively understand what is going on and where the problems are, they say.

This analyst has witnessed numerous cases wherein the CM manager, engineering manager or operations manager thought they understood what was going on in the processes. It was also apparent that they didn't agree about what the problems were, let alone agree on any given solution. When three folks involved in a process are asked to independently flow diagram that process, and come up with three different diagrams, what must we conclude? Ask two or more people, independently, how long the process typically takes from point X to point Y in work days? See if you get similar answers. Then measure from point X to Y and find that none of them is correct. When analyzing a company process, often more than one block diagram or flow diagram is presented – and they don't match.

If we are undertaking improvement to one of the processes, how are we to know if there is actually improvement or if things were made worse? If we don't measure all portions of the process, how do we know that our process improvement simply robbed Peter to pay Paul?

Isn't intelligent measurement and reporting a more reliable method than trusting our intuition or collective intuition? Isn't objective measurement better than subjective judgment?

Importance/urgency of metrics

In any given company, at any point in time, a given metric might be of more or less importance. This is true because it may indicate a serious need for control and/or improvement, indicate an "in-control" condition or indicate something in between. In this book, where practical, the importance or urgency of each report will thus be identified/discussed by the "Olympic method":

- **Gold** – highest importance/urgency
- **Silver** – medium importance/urgency
- **Bronze** – lowest importance/urgency.

Some charts and graphs will be identified by this method. Often, however, the importance of a metric will change over time. What is highest importance today may become of lower import as time passes – if improvement occurs. Also, what is of low importance today may well become more urgent over time. The reader, of course, should be the final determiner of this indicator. It is not suggested that the CM manager use this device on their metrics, only to have it in mind when deciding how often to prepare the report and what level of management to send it to.

In general the more urgent metric (Gold) would be distributed more frequently and the less important (Bronze) less frequently. The Gold metric would be sent to a higher level of management than the Bronze.

CM process ladder

Of course, measurements should normally be objective, but a few "measurement" methods may be totally subjective. One such subjective measurement is shown in Fig. 1.2. Place your company's processes and metrics on the CM process ladder.

Of course this "measurement" is intuitive and your estimate may not agree with others. It may be off a rung or more, but it is a place to start. If everyone agrees that your company is best in class or world class then there is probably no need to proceed with this book – if you have metrics to demonstrate that ranking.

Process quality

Throughout this work the speed of the processes will be emphasized. Speed is very important but not at the sacrifice of the quality of the process or of the documents. Yes, humans are prone to make 2–3% error when doing any job. The person downstream should be checking the work of the person upstream. In that manner we should be able to achieve 100% accuracy of engineering data. The downstream person is often, and should

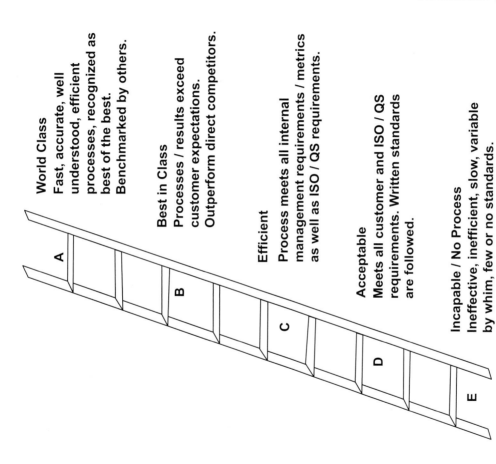

World Class
Fast, accurate, well understood, efficient processes, recognized as best of the best. Benchmarked by others.

Best in Class
Processes / results exceed customer expectations. Outperform direct competitors.

Efficient
Process meets all internal management requirements / metrics as well as ISO / QS requirements.

Acceptable
Meets all customer and ISO / QS requirements. Written standards are followed.

Incapable / No Process
Ineffective, inefficient, slow, variable by whim, few or no standards.

A

B

C

D

E

Figure 1.2 • CM process ladder.

be, the CM technician. They, the engineers and the management should not be satisfied with anything less than 100% accuracy of design data.

Above all it is essential to avoid setting up or continuing a process that encourages doing a job twice – once fast and again formally (correctly).

- **Principle:** The quality of the processes is paramount – we must speed up the processes but not hurry up to do it wrong.

Chapter Two

Metrics and process requirements

The terms "metric," "report" and "measurement" are sometimes used in this work interchangeably. Normally, however, the term "measurement" will refer to the gathering of data (charting), "metric" to the graphical presentation and "report" to the distribution of this knowledge in part or in total. A report thus might involve the data, the graphic presentation and/or text about the interpretation/significance/solution to the highlighted problem.

Metrics should not to be confused with the "metric system" of measurement or dimensioning. We are simply talking about gathering data about the processes, graphing/charting them and reporting on same.

The decisions as to what reports are best, who to distribute reports to, how frequently, and whether or not to send accompanying recommendations are all nagging issues. One must weigh the importance of the report, the time the recipients will have for analysis and always avoid the possibility of "baffling them with BS". This work will attempt to shed light on all these issues and more.

Timeliness of reporting

The initial creation of a metric/report should not wait for a problem to become painfully obvious. If at all possible, the metrics should be created first, to anticipate problems/issues.

The metric must also be distributed on a timely basis. A weekly report should be distributed on Monday or Tuesday of the following week, a monthly report in the first week of the following month, a daily report on the same day – don't go home until the report is distributed. Anything slower risks being cast aside as an "old newspaper" – thus the faster the better.

The first step to improvement

Before undertaking any process improvement, measure the related issue and prepare a graph and/or a chart. For example, if you are concerned about using up available part numbers, first figure out how many numbers are actually available (a six-digit part number without a tab/dash would yield 999,999 maximum available numbers) and how many have been used (see Table 2.1).

Part number usage

Plot that data on a timeline metric as in Fig. 2.1. The author uses Microsoft Excel® for both the data charting and the graphing/metric. They can also easily be done by hand drafting or with other, probably better, software tools.

Table 2.1 Measurement data – part number usage

Year	Cumulative PNs used
1	35,600
2	101,200
3	206,200
4	311,200
5	426,200
6	701,500
7	756,000
8	
9	999,999
10	

One can look at the graph for the first seven years and easily see that there is trouble ahead. Using the graph, it is easy to project "run-out" in year 9. This metric, in earlier years, would be considered Bronze or Silver but by the end of year 7 should be considered **Gold** because changing the part numbering system is difficult and far-reaching in any environment and little time remains to find and implement a fix for an issue of this magnitude.

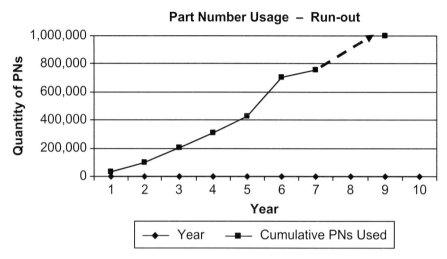

Figure 2.1 • Part number usage graphed.

The next step is to solve the problem. Are there part numbers unused that can be reclaimed? How many? Will a "where-used" search be required? How much time will that take? Can another digit be added to make a seven-digit number? Will all the legacy and planned software systems allow another digit? Should two more digits be added? Is this the time to add a tab/dash if none exists? Won't a trial/test of a seven/eight-digit number be required? Many questions need to be asked to guide a logical conclusion/solution.

The measurement data, the metric and suggested solution(s) should be put into a report to top management in year 8 or certainly very early in year 9. The report should be published at least once a month until a solution is agreed upon and implemented. Until a solution has been agreed upon and implemented, a hard copy of this metric and report should be placed in the hands or on the chair of key management people.

Not enough data/too much data

Many a CM manager has a file full of data and reports but no one seems to be listening to their warnings. It is critical that only key data be graphed and reported.

The part number usage issue could well be gathered and reported by mechanical, software and electrical departments. It could be done by part, assembly, reference document, etc. The gathering and display of such detail would only obfuscate the issue, however. This metric contains only one value – PN usage. Graphs with three values are less powerful, but can be absorbed by most viewers. More that three, in my experience, require too much study, even with color. The goal should be to, as vividly and concisely as possible, display the data that define the issue – easy for this analyst to say, but not always easy for you to do.

Sometimes the CM manager finds that they have data indicating problems but is frustrated because no one is listening. Sometimes they have too much data. For example, a typical change process may have 30 steps in it. If one were to measure the time between each step, the data would be overwhelming. Thus measuring the time between a few key points in the process is much more productive than measuring all 30 points.

Of course, the other extreme is not to gather any data and merely tell the management that based on your intuition a serious problem exists. If the management is likewise experienced and have the same intuition, this approach might work. Better, however, to chart/graph the issue. The graph in this case tends to impart a "sense of urgency." It also allows us to see if improvement occurs.

Metric formats

Data charts, graphs, pie diagrams, bar charts, Pareto charts, etc. all have a place in a metrics plan. The best choice for any given circumstance needs to be considered. Any of the variety of pictorial methods may be applicable. As you will see, this analyst tends to favor a timeline graph, preferably with goals set. Thus the timeline graph shows where we have been, where we are now, what the trend is and where we should be headed.

Using the timeline requires a decision to be made as to whether Saturday will be counted as a work day. A decision as to the time-frequency of the metric also needs to be made – daily, weekly or monthly.

Most of the suggested measurements will be done in whole work days. A more sophisticated approach, especially with flexible hours, might be to break the work day into ten hours/parts and measure to the tenth of a work day. This would better account for work days that are started early by some folks and ended late by others. Use of this technique would depend upon your hours and the need for precision.

Many companies designate calendar weeks into fiscal weeks – 13 to each fiscal quarter. This makes the length of each quarter essentially identical and thus comparisons of performance from quarter to quarter more meaningful.

If your software systems have "time tracking" and "report writer" ability you will probably have a head start on gathering measurement data.

Thru-put time

Regardless of the process being measured, the single most important metric we can measure is the process time, or "thru-put time." Time is money we say. One writer was more expansive: "**As a strategic weapon, time is the equivalent of money, productivity, quality, even innovation**" (*Harvard Business Review*: "Time – The Next Source of Competitive Advantage"). Think about it! Consult my *EDC Handbook* if you need details. Thus:

- **Principle:** The speed of your processes is critical to profitability!

The most important metric in any and all of the CM processes will be speed of the process. We are not talking about hurrying up to do it wrong; we are talking about taking the dwells or queues out of the process. Ask yourself what the "hands-on time" is for the tasks in a portion of the process. Then find out what the actual lapsed time is. Typically the lapsed time far exceeds the hands-on time. The time reduction is, thus, a matter of removing dwells/queues/dead time from the process, thus reducing the work in process and thus the process time.

Caution must be taken to assure that this doesn't mean "hurry up to do it wrong and therefore have to do it over again later." Many a company has instituted a "fast process" to be followed by the "formal" process. This is not speeding up the process but rather doing it twice, which is always the slowest method. This is exactly the process typically established by governments when they are bombarded with complaints about obtaining a license for example. They issue a temporary license to be followed later by the correct/formal license – doing the job twice.

Frequency of reporting

Shall a given metric be sent out once a day, week, month, or quarterly or yearly? Consider the importance of the information, the audience and the expected result.

What is the desired result? The part number usage metric might be sent only one time and the desired result obtained – the boss says that Charlie will fix the problem. The CM manager might send out a report with a suggested solution, specific action items expected of Information Technology, Materials, Supply Chain, etc. and ask for concurrence. Then obtain concurrence and implement the fix. This might be done in one or two months. Another company might need to report this metric monthly and possibly weekly for a year in order to get resolution.

Some metrics/reports are informational. In general, informational reports should be sent less frequently than those expecting action. Some horn-tooting may be in order. Some are to highlight a specific or critical problem. If the metric covers the backlog of change requests, and the trend is downward, current actions may be adequate and the metric sent less frequently – perhaps once a month. If the trend is upward and no corrective action is in place, a weekly metric including the measurement data and metric might be done to get folks' attention. Lacking any corrective action, the data, metric and suggested actions should be put together in a report for those involved.

In general, the Gold indicators must be distributed to the highest management levels. The Gold and Silver would be distributed to middle management and "all the above" to first-level management. Of course, key people should be included on all metrics and reports that involve them.

This analyst – the author – will generally suggest the frequency of each metric but that must be tempered by your circumstances. In general, only Gold metrics should be sent to executive management.

Policy and procedure requirements

Certain general "standards" should be available. This is a very important measure of merit for any product manufacturing company (see the *EDC Handbook* for more discussion of standards). Each process should have standards available and those will be suggested and listed in the applicable chapter. The following standards should be available for the CM system in general – check off those available, up to date and concisely written in your company:

Company Policy Statement – Outlines the CM "turf" and general responsibilities. Should include a page about the benefits of fast, accurate, well understood and measured processes.   Yes ☐   No ☐

Standard on Writing Standards – To obtain short, well-understood process documentation.   Yes ☐   No ☐

Product Specifications – Includes the content and format of critical product criteria that will be committed to the customer.   Yes ☐   No ☐

Drafting Standards – Includes allowable drawing and specification formats. Also covers EDC/CM requirements for content of design documents.   Yes ☐   No ☐

Doc Groups – List all company technical documents and define basic control responsibilities.   Yes ☐   No ☐

Cognizant (responsible) Engineers List – Defines the responsibilities of design engineers and others regarding the design and its documentation.   Yes ☐   No ☐

Part Numbers – Defines the attributes of the part number(s).   Yes ☐   No ☐

Tabulating Documents – Specifies company policy on tabulating documents and their control.   Yes ☐   No ☐

Approved Manufacturers List – Controls the acceptable manufacturers of a purchased item. May or may not contain the acceptable suppliers.   Yes ☐   No ☐

Teams – Defines the make-up of teams for each/every CM process.   Yes ☐   No ☐

Signatures – Specifies what functions should review and which should sign engineering and CM documents.   Yes ☐   No ☐

Prints, Point of Use, Paperless – Defines the company policy regarding distribution and control of design documents.   Yes ☐   No ☐

Class Coding/Naming Conventions/Group Technology – Specifies the company policy, procedure and standards to be used.   Yes ☐   No ☐

Nameplate and Serial Number – Defines the requirements for the nameplate drawing and serial number assignment.   Yes ☐   No ☐

Acronyms and Definitions Standard – Provides a single location for approved definitions and abbreviations in order to avoid placing them in every standard that requires them (see Chapter 11). Yes ☐ No ☐

Users Guide/CM Plan – Summarizes the CM standards for training company people, customers and suppliers. Yes ☐ No ☐

This list of general standards may not be adequate for some companies but it is certainly more complete than found in most companies. A best of the best practices CM standards manual is available from the author.

Work in process (WIP) and thru-put time

If we measured the number of documents done per month (in any part of any process) and counted the number of docs in process (work in process – WIP), we could estimate the probable doc process time.

Example: We count 20 new docs in drafting from point X to point Y. If we typically complete ten new documents per month, the probable thru-put time is about two months ($20 \div 10 = 2$).

Recognizing this basic "formula" we can see that there are two ways of improving the speed of any process:

1. Taking the dwells out of the process as mentioned above by measurement and process improvement.
2. Reducing the WIP – if we cut the WIP in half (to ten docs in process) the thru-put time would go down to one month.

WIP reduction can be achieved by various means without process improvement – working overtime, added manpower, temporary manpower, farm-out of some work, even rejection/elimination of the need for some documents. Such "one-time" projects sometimes work. One company worked all their technical folks (the VP of Engineering included himself and all managers) to work off the WIP. They had measured the incoming and outgoing rates and found them very similar. They reduced their new drawing time from several weeks to a few days.

In any WIP reduction project, caution should be taken to measure the input and output rates to assure that they are about the same. If the input is exceeding the output, we need to either increase the manpower dedicated, reject incoming work or improve the process.

Thus, it is very important to measure and track the WIP for any CM process – not only as a quick way to estimate the thru-put time (as we will do here) but for better forecasting of the probable trend of the measured thru-put time. This rough adaptation of the Queuing Theory can be used for any process when and if:

- The normal/average completion volume (the output of ten per month) is known and relatively constant
- The input and output rates are approximately equal
- The "content" of the WIP is fairly consistent – docs are not mostly "easy" or mostly "very difficult"; or very many have not been in process for a long time.

If any of the above is not the case, the estimation will be faulty. It is, however, undeniable that WIP and time are directly related: more WIP, more time; less WIP, less time. Thus the process thru-put time is directly proportional to the WIP. Therefore the WIP and output count method can be used as a rough estimating tool for thru-put time. Although the thru-put time should be measured document by document (release, request, change, BOM, deviation, etc.) the WIP/count method can be used to identify problem areas. If your resources are limited and measuring/logging the thru-put of a process is therefore impractical, at the very least use the WIP/count method to identify a few processes or portions of processes that need doc-by-doc measurement.

Let's take another example. We may be of the mind that the deviation process lapsed time is excessive. Once a week, at the same time each week, count the total deviations in process and count those completed that week. Let's say that 20 deviations were completed that week and 38 were in process. We can approximate the process thru-put time at $38 \div 20 = 1.9$ weeks lapsed time. If we repeat that process each week for a quarter, our data would appear (using 20 completions per week for simplicity) as in Table 2.2.

We can graph that data showing vividly what has happened to the WIP count, but not so vividly what happens to the thru-put time (see Fig. 2.2).

We can also combine the chart and graph to better see what happens to the thru-put time numbers. This picture is still an approximation of the thru-put time. We can now see that when the WIP bottoms out the probable thru-put time is at its minimum – one half-week (see Fig. 2.3).

Finally, an approximation of the thru-put time based upon the same data but simplified to the most important bit of data – time – is shown in Fig. 2.4.

You will notice that the deviation process speed decreased over time to a half-week, but then increased toward the early poorer performance. If one half-week thru-put time was once achievable, it should probably be sustainable. Analysis is required to find causes and solutions. A WIP reduction program may be sufficient but it is likely that some fundamental process change is required.

Table 2.2 Probable thru-put time if about 20 completions per week

GOLD		
Week	WIP count	Probable thru-put time in weeks
1	38	1.90
2	35	1.75
3	30	1.50
4	27	1.35
5	26	1.30
6	26	1.30
7	21	1.05
8	15	0.75
9	10	**0.50**
10	18	0.90
11	27	1.35
12	29	1.45
13	32	1.60

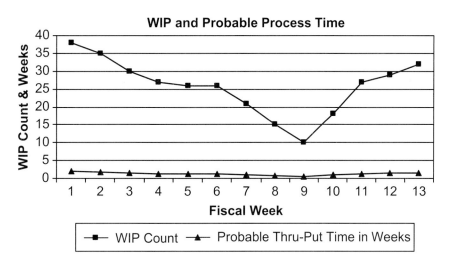

Figure 2.2 • Graph of probable thru-put time if 20 completions per week.

In order to be precise, each document would need to be measured from start to complete. This would get the word "probable" out of the metric.

One could measure and report the above conditions by publishing all four reports above (Table 2.2, Figs 2.2–2.4). This would, by this author's estimation, be considerable overkill – TIM (too much information). Publishing only Fig. 2.4 (probable thru-put time) would most simply highlight the problem and would therefore be ideal for getting management's attention.

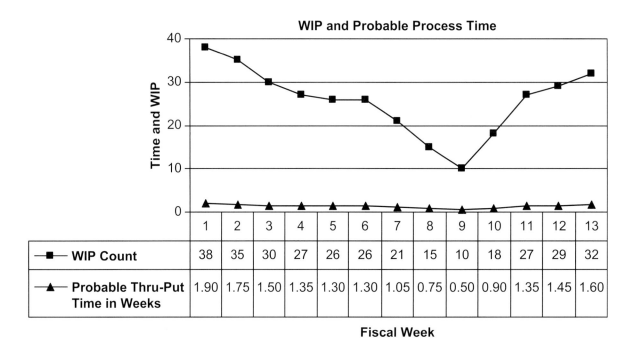

Figure 2.3 • Chart and graph of probable thru-put time if 20 completions per week.

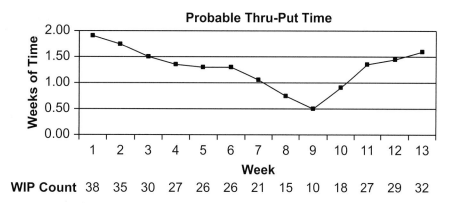

Figure 2.4 • Probable thru-put time via weekly WIP and completions count.

Getting management's attention

Management folks are usually very busy people. They put in many extra hours, as some other folks do. They are generally inundated with emails, snail mail, reports, budget information, personal matters and much more. So what is the most effective way to get their attention?

• **Principle:** Send less, not more.

Don't only use email if there is an important issue. Make a hard copy of the metric and hand it to each manager involved. If they aren't in their office, leave it on their chair. Write a note on it. Attach recommendations to it if appropriate. Do not skip levels of management. Inform each level that you are distributing the particular metric or report to their boss. Show the distribution on the metric/report itself. Ask them if they saw the report if you see them in the hall. If time allows, explain what you are doing or what should be done about a highlighted problem. Listen carefully to what they have to say and act upon it.

Do your metrics in color but do not use color to present TMI – too much information. The metrics in this book which aren't easily presented/viewed in black and white may be found in color by accessing http://www.elsevierdirect.com/companion.jsp?ISBN=9780080964454

If you are tooting your own horn or your improvement team's horn, readily admit it. Remember that management is looking for people who can identify *and* solve problems – not present the problem to the management and expect them to solve it. There are all too many people around that can recognize and highlight problems but too few who can solve them.

Management champion

Try to find a management champion, one high-level manager for all the CM processes or one for the process you think most needs improvement – an executive management VP or director. Educate that person as to how the metrics can help highlight and improve perceived problems. Make key metrics and distribute them. Lobby for a champion. Improving processes without a management champion can be done, but it is much easier with a champion (see the *EDC Handbook* for more on this subject).

Training metrics

This analyst is often confronted with situations wherein the processes are poorly understood – sometimes by the CM folks but more frequently by their internal customers. Too little time is spent/available for training the people involved in the CM processes. My recommendations almost always include dedication of more time/manpower for training. On occasion a comment will be made about the fact that training is expensive. I always agree, but point out that if one thinks training is expensive, **try ignorance!**

The CM managers and their key people should be spending a significant amount of time getting trained themselves and in training others. Unfortunately few benchmarks exist in this area but this analyst's experience would say that at least 10% of all CM hours available should be spent in training or giving training. CM folks should all keep track of those hours and the CM manager should total the time and report to themselves and the boss. In a larger company a full-time trainer to also coordinate and facilitate training is probably a wise investment.

Each person would have to keep track of time spent in and giving training and their total hours worked. What work is considered training should be defined – giving group presentations, one-on-one training, seminars, reading books or online, etc. The CM manager would summarize this data monthly. One good method of presenting this data is shown in Fig. 2.5.

This metric was labeled Bronze simply because there is no apparent need to distribute it beyond the CM group and their manager – who hopefully is the Chief Engineer. The trend in this case is positive. A goal should probably be set to achieve a total of at least 10% training time.

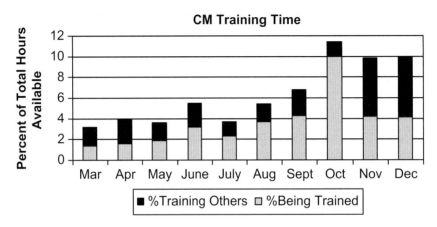

Figure 2.5 • CM training hours as a percentage of total hours.

Another CM unique measurement might be time spent doing process audits. This could be a separate chart or added to the above chart. Each year at least one major process should be audited. Are the processes written, concise, clear, followed and measured?

Setting goals

Facts are important and metrics showing facts are worthwhile but somewhat lacking without goals and plans for improvement. Set modest goals unless you have an improvement project backed by a high-level manager.

If the change process time is 40 days from process points X to Y and the CM manager or their management wishes to see that time be five work days, then set that goal immediately and let all involved know what the goal is and what plan of action you have.

The goal should usually have a date for planned accomplishment – five work days by the end of the next ten months for example. Allow a realistic timeframe for that to be achieved based on your own time, the team time and management champion involvement.

If you are improving the processes yourself or with an ad hoc team, without high-level management's direct involvement, then you might start with a goal of 30 days within ten months. When achieved, reflect on what the next goal might be. In other words, without high-level management backing, set the goals in small steps so as not to become too discouraged.

Tooting your horn

A little well-placed horn-tooting is not a bad idea. As an old boss of this writer once said: "A train doesn't run by its whistle, but you never saw a train without a whistle." His clear meaning – if you don't toot your own horn now and then, your train/team may not be heard when it needs to be.

One way to do this is to have a lunch meeting to celebrate a goal reached. Invite the boss and management champion and send an email to key people and management touting the success. Give lots of credit to your team and anyone who helped. Another effective way to do some horn tooting is to have a party – perhaps when larger goals are met. Again invite the team, anyone who helped and the key management people.

Quickly summarize where you were, where you are now and where you are going. Again, give much/most/all the credit to the team and those who helped.

- **Principle:** When it is horn-honking time, honk the team's horn, not your own!

Facts database

Some companies undertake process improvements without any of the metrics described in this book. Some also neglect some basic fact-finding. Both are a risky approach to process improvement. At the very least, a few major metrics should be put in place before starting. Also, a facts database – benchmarking your own process – would be a good idea.

This writer suggests that a database of facts about the process(es) should be developed by random sampling of the historical forms involved and extracting all practical data. It is all too easy to think that one knows what percentage of changes are "document only" changes, for example. This will avoid making decisions about the process, policy or workflow based on erroneous assumptions.

The sample need not be scientific – it might be just 10% or the last six months of forms involved, every tenth ECO for example. A spreadsheet of the data, properly summarized, is a highly desirable tool. If we are going to improve the change process, in addition to implementing the key metrics, sample the ECO forms for:

- Class – doc only, interchangeable, non-interchangeable
- Type – meet product specs, reduce cost, exceed specs (improvement)
- Impacts (yes or no) – regulator(s), software, firmware, tools, fixtures, test equipment, assembly process, suppliers, packaging, publications, product spec, fabrication process, etc.

- Affects – make items, buy items, both
- Impacts – electrical, mechanical, hydraulic, pneumatic, software, etc.
- Customer approvals/notification required
- FCO required – recall, on failure, etc.
- Effectivity traced – SN, date, other
- Number of parts, assemblies, specifications, parts lists affected
- Number of mark-ups and from–to descriptions
- Revision level change, PN change, both
- Number of new documents involved
- Old part disposition – use up, scrap, return to supplier, reworkable, reworked yes/no
- Number of signatures – on mark-ups, on ECO, on BOM list, etc.
- Dates tracked (start, design complete, etc.).

These data should be summarized and averaged. It will be of an enormous help when designing process flow, forms, form instruction, standards and policy improvements.

Benchmarking

This analyst did a comprehensive survey of companies that had representatives attend his seminars. Fifty-eight companies/divisions participated. Over 100 questions were asked and answers given about the organization, processes, workflow, forms, volume, thru-put time, etc. Comparing your operations to other companies' is a huge benefit to any company. For this reason the author is including the benchmarking survey results in applicable chapters.

To the best of the author's knowledge this is the *first and only quantitative product manufacturing study in our discipline*. The questions, summary results and the author's comments are included in applicable chapters. Company-specific information has not, is not and will not be disclosed. All respondents were seminar attendees. A few have also been clients of EC^3 Corp. – the author's company.

The survey was done in late 1995 and throughout 1996 into 1997 and summarized in early 1997. The results are based on subsequent questioning in seminars and on consulting jobs, and are still generally valid except as noted.

Survey participants

The participants described their products as follows: detection devices, jet engines, telecom, metrology, rock crushers, hotel communication, aircraft and antennas, hose and ducts, mail machines, broadcast antenna, batteries, wheelchairs, medical devices, rail and mass transit, digital radios, physics education, equipment to mfg optic lenses, microwave hybrid, membrane keyboards, video systems, PC disk drives, automation components, industrial heating systems, auto and appliance controls, control/inspect gauging equipment, truck hydraulic lifts, wafer track, irrigation sprinklers and valves, time/temp. humidity instruments, HVAC controls, tele multimedia, batteries and chargers, high-end print inspection and counterfeit detection equipment, telecom switching, diagnostic and test equipment, mechanical assemblies, liquid level measurement, airplane windows and lenses, medical diagnostic, capital process equipment, induction heating, auto brakes (pumps), fuel injection, wiring devices, RF/M-wave power amplifiers, automotive lamps, children's toys, respiratory protection, refrigerated food cases, circuit protection, network analysis test equipment, machine tool components, CPM capital equipment/ICs, adhesives and sealants, medical products, electronics.

More information about the participant companies is in the survey details that follow.

Survey results

The survey general questions and answers follow. Other portions of the survey are included in applicable chapters. Where appropriate, charts have been used. When raw numbers are given they may not add up to the 58 contributors because some didn't answer that question. When percentages are given they were based upon only those who did respond to that question. In those cases where more than one choice could be made, the percentages may add up to more than 100%.

Benchmarking survey – general

For comparison the applicable portion of the benchmarking survey is as follows:

All questions answered for your:
   Division 43%
   Company 57%.

Name you call your EDC/CM group:

   22 – Documentation or Doc Control

   6 – Configuration Management or Control

   6 – Engineering Service/Support

   4 – Drafting or Design

   20 – Other (many and various).

Comment: In recent years many more companies have used the Configuration Management name.

Number of people in company or division (see Fig. 2.6):

   0–100 = 17%

   101–500 = 55%

   501–1000 = 9%

   Over 1000 = 19%.

Production/ship rate (units per month – all products; see Fig. 2.7):

   0–10 = 12%

   11–100 = 12%

   101–1000 = 20%

   1001–10,000 = 22%

   Over 10,000 = 34%.

Number of People in Co / Div

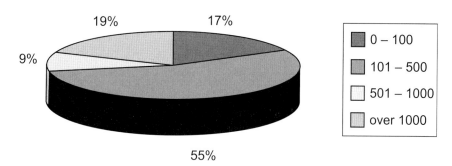

Figure 2.6 • Size of company or division (number of people).

Production Ship Rate

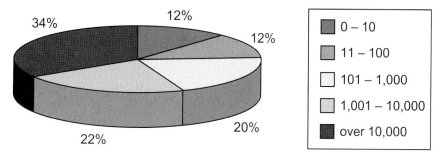

Figure 2.7 • Production/ship rate (units per month – all products).

Manufacturing sites:

33 – one site

4 – two sites

6 – three sites

10 – four or more.

Design engineering sites:

40 – one site

9 – two sites

5 – three or more sites.

Design and manufacturing:

27 are in the same building

11 different cities

7 different countries

8 combination of the above

7 same site

7 same city, different sites.

Comment: May check more than one choice.

Number of people in CM group (including manager if full-time): see Fig. 2.8.

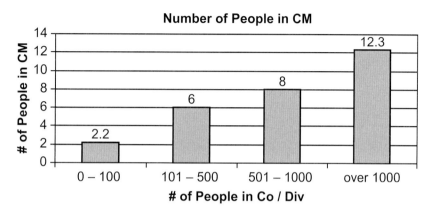

Figure 2.8 • People in the CM group (including manager if full-time).

EDC/CM group responsible for (check all applicable):
Design docs 100%
Manufacturing docs 59%
Publications docs 36%
Other docs 38%.

Derived from examining individual answers:
29% only engineering docs
21% all technical docs.

41

Comment: Didn't ask how many require all documents affected by a change to be "bundled" in the same change – a poor practice in this analyst's experience.

Who CM organization answers to (see Fig. 2.9):

Engineering 67%
Manufacturing 17%
QA 9%
Other 5%
President 2%.

Comment: Answering to the President – that's clout!

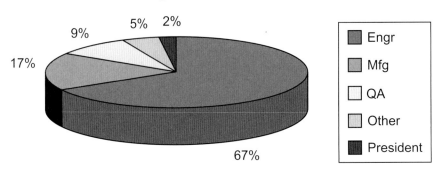

CM Organization Answers To

Figure 2.9 • Who in the organization the CM group answers to (pick one).

Opinion – Value of the CM discipline is generally understood in our company:
Yes 53%
No 47%.
Comment: Appreciation for the CM discipline has increased significantly since the survey.

Levels of management from CM upward (include EDC/CM manager up to and including the division or company head):
Average 3.5
Range 1–9.
Comment: Should be no more than company/division head – first; chief engineer – second; engineering services/CM – third.

Products are (check all applicable):
Electrical 90%
Mechanical 95%
Hydraulic 24%
Chemical 17%
Pneumatic 28%
Other 9% (plastic/biological prevalent).
Comment: Two respondents added software – should have asked specifically about software.

Each product has a released product specification:
Yes 56%
No 44%.

Comment: Some might not have recognized a catalog as a product specification or may not use the term. It does surprise the author, even after defining the term, how many don't have such a document. How do companies without a product spec know what to design to, test to, etc.?

Can non-interchangeable change content be determined by nameplate data:

Yes

No

What data is needed?

Comment: Question was poorly asked – should have said "with" or "from"! Results are thus not usable.

Product safety specifications (see Fig. 2.10):

Understood 52%

Written by product 31%

One for all products 15%

Both ways 2%.

Comment: Unwritten/understood safety specs – hope they don't end up in court. Do labels on a product substitute for safety specifications?

Product nameplate contains:

SN 66%

Lot number 14%

Date code 55%

Product number 55%

Product Safety Specifications

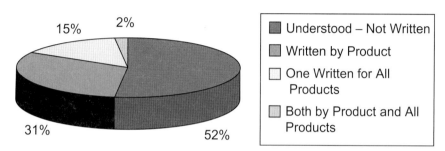

Figure 2.10 • Product safety specifications.

Top part number 38%
Mod./rev. code 28%.

Rev. code on the nameplate is the top drawing rev.:
Yes 94%
No 6%.
Comment: Are folks rolling revs up to and including the top drawing?

Regulated by (check all applicable):
Good commercial practices 57%
UL/CSA/OSHA, etc. 50%

FDA/GMP 17%
DOD/MIL specs 17%
FAA/JAA 10%
NASA 3%
Other (DOH, VDE, DIN, DOT, FCC, NIOSH, SSPA, EN 71, ANSI, NACE, ASTM) 16%.

Forms used (see Fig. 2.11):
　　One for release, request and change 19%
　　One for request and change 14%
　　Two: one for release, one for request and change 28%
　　Two: one for request, one for release and change 33%
　　Other 6%.
Comment: It can be assumed that forms other than release, request and change forms are prevalent. For example, many companies have a fast change form, most have a deviation/waiver form, etc.

EDC process(es) are documented:
　　Yes 45%
　　No 24%
　　Partly 31%
　　Quantity of forms 3.4 average
　　Quantity of form instructions 1.9 average
　　Quantity of procedures 3.2 average

Number of Forms Used

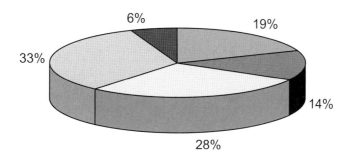

Figure 2.11 • Form(s) used.

Quantity of flow diagrams 1.9 average
Quantity of policies 1.3 average
Quantity of standards 1.1 average.

Approximate total pages of EDC/CM process delineation: 32.5 pages average.

Comment: Author's standards are 76 pages (45 standards). Every form should have a form instruction.

ISO 9000 certified:
Yes 16%
No 38%
In process 43%
No intent 3%.

Certifying organization: _____. Est. cost $ _____
Comment: Not enough respondents to give meaningful summary as to certifiers or cost. More recent polling in seminars indicates that 85/90% are now ISO certified. Occasionally a few companies have now indicated they are allowing their certification to lapse.

Other portions of the survey are included in applicable chapters.

Chapter Three

New item release

The "release" of a new item (part, assembly, document, software or product) is simply the act of moving the item and its documentation from one phase of the lifecycle to the next – typically development, pilot and production. Thus the product finally moves to the marketplace and begins to make profit for the company. Making this happen fast, accurately, and at minimum cost is critical to any manufacturing company's profitability.

This process *excludes* new items required for a change. If a new item or document is required for a change, it should be released as part of the change – in the applicable ECO document.

The release process can and should be measured in its parts and in total – the total time to bring a new product to market.

Release standards, definitions and rules

Of course, the meaning of "release" must be carefully defined in the CM standards. For example, release of a part must include or be preceded by release of its material spec and any other applicable specs. Another example: the release of an assembly must mean that all of its materials, parts, part specifications and the assembly specifications are included or have been previously released. In other words, the release should occur from the "bottom up" – in lead time (see the *EDC Handbook* for detailed definition).

If your company has a Release to Pilot and a Release to Production, which it probably should, the rules should hold true for both. The charts and graphs should be done for both. The CM standards needed for the release process are:

Release Policy – Contains requirements as mentioned above. Yes ☐ No ☐

Teams in Release – Specific meeting time, membership, chair, action items, etc. noted. Yes ☐ No ☐

Release Form – If different than the Change Form. Yes ☐ No ☐

Form Instruction – Box-by-box instructions for completing the form for item release. If electronic a "cursor pop-up" may be used. Yes ☐ No ☐

Phase Release Chart/Diagram – Specifies phases expected and the detailed requirements for each phase. Yes ☐ No ☐

Release Flow Diagram – Delineates the release procedure in flow diagram form. Yes ☐ No ☐

New product time to market

In the broadest sense, CM should measure the overall performance of the new product release teamwork and the process by comparing product to product over time – the weeks/months to bring each product to market. This should be done by major phase – not in too much detail (see the *EDC Handbook* for further definition).

For the Front End Loader product family let's presume that the baseline (first) product release time was measured by phases – and that subsequent "spin-off" products (FEL-100 and FEL-200) are similarly measured. We can then chart the progress (see Table 3.1).

Table 3.1 New product time to market

GOLD				
Phase	**Phase description**	**Baseline**	**FEL-100**	**FEL-200**
I	From product start, to all docs released for pilot	4.1 months	3.5 months	3.0 months
II	From all docs released for pilot to pilot units completed	4.3 months	3.1 months	2.2 months
III	From pilot units complete to all docs released to production	2.3 months	2.1 months	
IV	From production release to first production unit	3.5 months	2.2 months	
	Time to market	14.2 months	10.9 months	

If the design teams are performing properly, *learning from the prior team's experience* and if the process is being continuously improved, similar products should be released in less time for each subsequent release – boy, that's a lot of "ifs." Of course, without measurement we won't know whether or not there is improvement.

Notice that the release process has been divided into four phases. These phases and the terminology vary widely but the basic concept is critical – not too many phases or TMI (too much information) results.

This is a long-term metric that should be kept and distributed each time a new bit of data is added. It is a critical measurement, should be distributed at the highest levels of management and remain perpetually Gold. Highlighting the new data (since the metric was last published) may be in order.

To be sophisticated with this metric, we might add a line to the chart to indicate the percentage of new/unique part numbers in the product. This would allow us to put the time to release in perspective.

Also important to this metric would be a measurement of the number of changes to each new product in the first year of its existence. This would tell us whether or not we hurried up to do it wrong – a process quality indicator.

Thus, over time, tracking of the following data might be in order (see Table 3.2).

Notice that the last two products have not been in production for a year and thus the change data are not yet available. We can still analyze these data and learn some very important lessons. For example, FEL-200 was developed and released in record time but also with record changes in the first year of production. This probably required more service effort and possibly more field changes. If this was a conscious decision, the

Table 3.2 Time to market comparison

GOLD

	Product type, FEL							
	0	**100**	**101**	**150**	**200**	**202**	**210**	**220**
Total time to market (months)	14.2	10.9	11.3	10.2	8.9	10.4	9.1	8
Percentage of unique part numbers	42	27	26	19	28	16	22	20
Number of changes in first year	87	63	54	37	83	28		

service was fast and done with little interruption to the customers; then goals were met. If this was a "hurry up and do it wrong" with customers angry, then the record release time was counter-productive.

If you (or your audience) are good at analyzing numbers the chart in Table 3.2 may be sufficient to highlight possible issues. If you aren't of the "bean counter" mentality, a picture would be better for you (see Fig. 3.1). Note that the products are charted in the sequence of release and thus the chart is in "rough time sequence".

From this metric we can see that the time to market is decreasing but sometimes at the apparent sacrifice of increased changes such as in the FEL-200 release.

You may have noticed that FEL-200 also had more unique part numbers than other recent products. This certainly could have been a contributor to the increase in the first year changes but probably not sufficient to

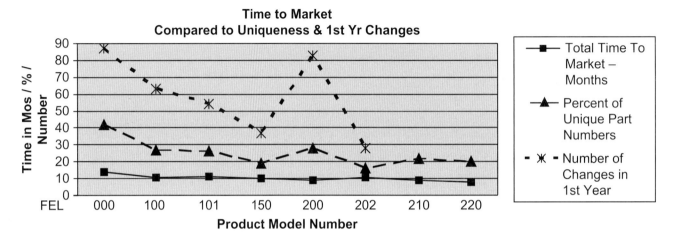

Time to Market
Compared to Uniqueness & 1st Yr Changes

Legend:
- ■ Total Time To Market – Months
- ▲ Percent of Unique Part Numbers
- ✳ Number of Changes in 1st Year

Y-axis: Time in Mos / % / Number

X-axis: Product Model Number — FEL, 000, 100, 101, 150, 200, 202, 210, 220

Figure 3.1 ● Time to market comparisons.

cause the magnitude of change activity measured. Whatever the cause, it was apparently taken care of in the FEL-202 development.

One electronic product company found increasing volume of changes occurring because the team review of drawings had been abandoned in the release process in order to move the product to market faster. They tried "online approvals" of the release document rather than face-to-face review/signing of the drawings and specifications. When they decided to return to face-to-face review again the change volume again decreased.

Release process flow diagram

Each individual design document release should occur by a specified process. The individual releases should occur in lead time to buy or build. The "individual release" might be for one document, one item, a group of items, a module of code, an assembly, part of an assembly, etc. It might be done by a unique document or by an entry in a "blanket document." It might be done either online, by manual or both. But it should always be done in lead time to manufacture.

In this analyst's experience the face-to-face document review should also not be abandoned. A document should not be allowed to pass the "release test" unless all the referenced documents are or have been released. An assembly should not be allowed to be released unless all of its components have been released.

The process should be flow diagrammed and measured. The diagram shown here is a "worst case" release flow. Thus, certain documents might not go thru all steps in the process. Release of a referenced document would not be "modeled and tested," for example. For the "worst case" flow, see Fig. 3.2.

Notice that this particular flow has 13 steps or events. The events which are to be measured are shown in rectangles *and* have a "clock" attached. The rectangles with the clock highlight the significant events to be measured and thus avoid the clutter of data that would result from measuring all 13 steps – this avoids TMI.

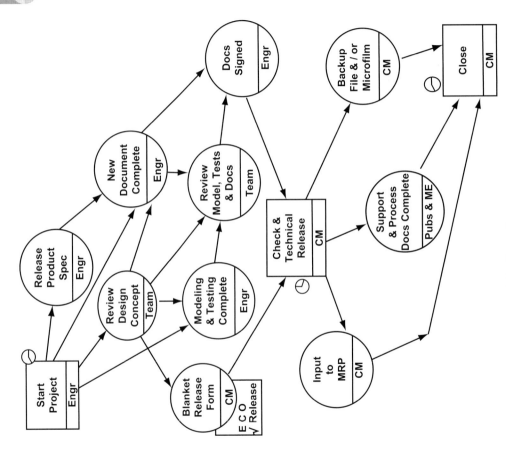

Figure 3.2 • Release activity flow diagram.

Release activity data

Each release would be, in this diagram, considered a separate "project" and separately measured. The "start project/start date" can be measured on the honor system (ask the engineer to enter on the release for when he/she actually started. More sophisticated methods can be developed by the team – for example, the team can agree as to when a "project" should be started in order to stay on lead time according to the development schedule.

A "project" might be a casting drawing, the machined drawing and all related design specifications. It might be a purchase specification for a component. The team should determine the logical "projects."

Data should be kept on each release action – whether it is done on a separate form, an entry on a "blanket" release, or done by an online routing. This data should include at least the information shown in Table 3.3.

The data created in this chart were made up for example purposes. It contains the releases actually completed in January. In this example they were also all started in January – your data would not be so simplistic.

Totaling and averaging all *completions* and *only completions* in the month, regardless of when they were started, is probably the best method to use for your metric.

A decision needs to be made as to whether Saturday will be counted as a work day. A decision as to the frequency of the metric also needs to be made. In our case, monthly was deemed sufficient because the process seems to be under control and within reasonable limits.

These data indicate that the measurement is done in whole days. As mentioned before, a more sophisticated approach with flexible hours worked might be to break the work day into ten hours/parts and measure to the tenth of a work day.

Table 3.3 January release activity data collection

BRONZE

Release number	Start date	Tech release date	Complete date	Work days start to tech release	Work days tech release to complete	Total work days	Number of docs released
1243	1/5	1/8	1/10	3	2	5	3
1244	1/6	1/11	1/13	5	2	7	17
1245	1/2	1/7	1/8	5	1	6	8
1246	1/7	1/15	1/18	8	3	11	1
1247	1/1	1/20	1/24	20	4	24	14
			Total	41	12	53	43
		Ave. per release		8.2	2.4	10.6	8.6

One could certainly track more events or keep the data by kind of document – part, assembly, reference, electrical, mechanical, etc. Doing so, however, would probably enter the realm of TMI and the viewer's eyes would glaze over.

Notice that the time and volume are averaged for January release action completions:

- 8.2 work days from start to tech release
- 2.4 work days from tech release to complete
- Totaling an average of 10.6 work days
- An average of 8.6 documents per release.

These data, standing alone, are not of much use. If we compare them to previous history, however, they will become much more meaningful. Are we getting better or worse over time?

Release activity summary

The key information can now be added to prior months. In this case, we will show the current month and the last 11 months – dropping January of last year (see Table 3.4).

This measurement chart is treated as Bronze because the current data indicate a fairly fast process. In January of last year this metric should have been labeled Gold because the process time was, for most environments, very slow. During the year it should have changed to Silver and now to Bronze.

Since the average time to make an individual release is so significant to getting the product to market in the least time, this metric could well be treated as Gold in perpetuity.

Table 3.4 Chart of release data by month

BRONZE

Month	Ave. work days start to tech release	Ave. work days tech release to close	Total ave. work days	Ave. docs per release
Feb	22.5	10.6	33.1	14.6
Mar	24.6	9.7	34.3	16.8
April	21.1	8.2	29.3	12.7
May	19.2	8.9	28.1	13.9
June	19.7	7.3	27.0	12.2
July	16.3	7.0	23.3	11.9
Aug	14.8	5.6	20.4	11.2
Sept	12.1	4.9	17.0	10.4
Oct	12.7	5.2	17.9	9.8
Nov	10.5	3.9	14.4	8.6
Dec	9.7	2.9	12.6	9.1
Jan	8.2	2.4	10.6	8.6

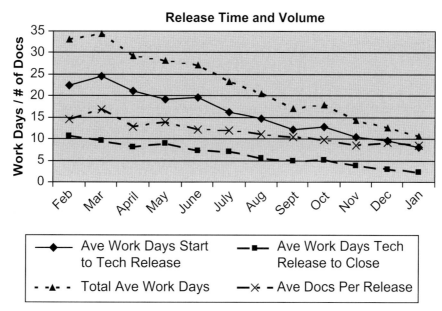

Figure 3.3 • Release time and volume graph.

We could now plot that data by month in a graph for somewhat easier analysis (see Fig. 3.3).

If you reference this graph in color it is fairly readable, although still somewhat confusing because four plotted series of data make for a little clutter.

Release – sorting out what's important

The total average release time is probably the most important metric from the data collected. One company viewed early data showing the total time in the 35-work-day range and determined to establish an improvement team and set a goal to reduce the overall time to ten work days by the end of the year. As you can see, the goal was effectively reached at the end of January – still, very good results (see Fig. 3.4).

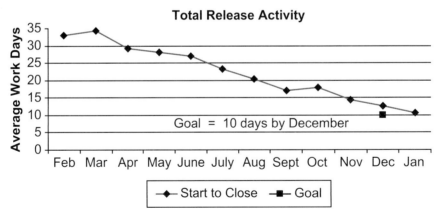

Figure 3.4 • Total release time with goal.

Notice that the more simplistic the graph, the more powerful the message. We could also sort out another of the two most important measurements in this case – total average work days and average documents per release – for another important, powerful and simplistic management report (see Fig. 3.5).

We may well think that these two measurements are very important and see some correlation. The implication is that the fewer documents per release, the shorter the release time – divide and conquer. This is no doubt true in this writer's experience *but much more must happen in order to drive down the average time to release*. In order to attain short process time performance, there must be much more occurring than merely putting a policy in place to release in smaller batches.

This metric may well, therefore, be misleading. A significant continuous improvement team effort is usually required to attain this kind of improvement. It certainly was in the company used as the model here.

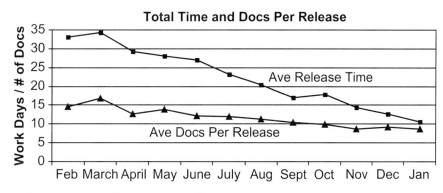

Figure 3.5 • Total release time compared to docs per release.

Their change process time was measured first and deemed excessive. The goal was set and that time was driven down by a significant improvement project with management backing.

Surprisingly the improvement first sought and obtained was in the *change* process. Their engineers knew how slow and painful the change process was and were therefore reluctant to release anything. They did so only in batches after they were very comfortable with the design. After the change process time was reduced significantly, the engineers were thus not hesitant to release a document because it was so relatively easy to change. They were therefore much more willing to release in lead time to buy or build. This analyst has seen this phenomenon many times. Thus:

- **Principle:** Make sure that your *change* process is fast, accurate, measured and well understood prior to attempting improvement in the release process.

Another meaningful metric would show the average time from start to tech release and from tech release to close – again, in this example, excluding the time to release the support and process documents (see Fig. 3.6).

An explanation for the positive trend may not be evident – process improvements, overtime, temporary manpower and/or other possibilities may be in play. It should be important to the management, so add a note to the metric or attach a report to explain the trend. The note might be horn-tooting – "improvement team getting results."

The total release time could be plotted on this graph, but that is probably TMI – and we had another graph (Fig. 3.5) to show that metric with the documents per release.

The number of releases (release count in the month) may be considered important and plotted or entered as raw data below the X-axis. This analyst cares much more about the documents per release than the

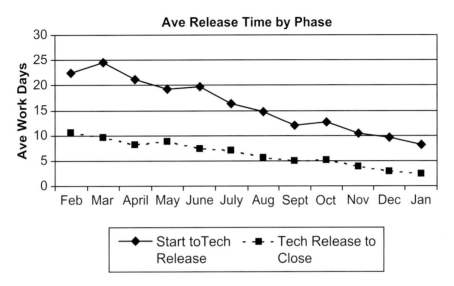

Figure 3.6 • Average release time by phase.

number of them. If someone says "we have too many releases," tell them it is the release time and release in lead time that are important, not the quantity of releases. Batching releases is, in fact, generally counter-productive. This is not to say that a "blanket release" cannot be wisely used – with each release logged on the blanket.

In any event, the trend in this case is very positive and some horn-tooting may be in order.

65

Development process case study

One company chief engineer was of the mind that the development process was too long. The process was divided into three major parts – design, drafting and approval. They found that each part took approximately the same amount of time – ten work days, a month and a half total. The chief engineer began to question the approval process. It was found that five people signed the typical document – in series – and they were all in the Design Engineering organization. No one representing the document users was signing.

The design engineer, the design drafter, a checker, the engineering manager and the engineering director all signed. After considerable analysis and soul searching, they determined to have two signatures – the responsible engineer and a manufacturing engineer representing both make and buy needs. This didn't mean that the engineer's managers could not and did not review the documents.

It seemed that engineers were comfortable with so many signatures – "they can't fire all of us." The engineering managers were largely rubber stamps. The CM department was given checking responsibility and made part of the design team, as was the manufacturing engineer. The checkers were moved to CM. The result was a reduction of nine work days in total – seven from the approval time and two from the drafting time.

They kept track of the changes per document in the following months and found a decline in the revision activity.

Release in lead time

One of the most important release metrics is a comparison of the *required release date to the actual release date*. In order to meet the product release schedule, when must the item be released in order to build or buy, inspect, issue, etc.? If the item is to be purchased, the Supply Chain people should be able to tell us when that item needs to be released to prevent scheduled delivery slippage. If the item is to be made in-house the manufacturing folks should be able to do the same. In fact, they will have to enter these lead-time data into the MRP/ERP system sooner or later, so let's do it sooner. The company should have one or two who are good at estimating lead time and do it earlier rather than later. At Brand X, a grizzled engineer in the Industrial Engineering Department estimated both cost and lead time for make and buy items. If the cost is included in this estimation, then the product cost will also be known much earlier than normal.

If the new product has 40 new proprietary designed items they should be entered in the BOM and given estimated lead times so that the engineer and the team can address each change in lead time to buy or build. The team would thus feed the design engineer the *needed* release date for the new product's unique items in lead-time order – so every effort can be made to release them in lead-time order.

Let's just take the first dozen of those items, for example. Extract the lead time for those items, convert that to the date required and compare that to the actual date released. Chart those data (see Table 3.5).

In this example, as you can see, there were eight items released after the needed release date. Four were released ahead of the required date. Releasing ahead of schedule is okay, provided we don't rob Peter to pay Paul.

Table 3.5 Lead-time performance measurement

GOLD				
Item	**Item description**	**Lead time (weeks)**	**Work days after need**	**Work days before need**
1	Base casting	42	10	
2	Left forging	38		9
3	Rear casting	36	9	
4	Molded front panel	35		12
5	Right forging	33	11	
6	Molded left brace	30	5	
7	Molded right brace	27	1	
8	Molded side panel	23		6
9	Molded back panel	21	7	
10	G2 gear stamping	18	4	
11	G1 gear stamping	15	2	
12	Machined gear shaft	13		5

That is, perhaps we put resources into item(s) released ahead of the needed date that should have been put into those items behind the needed date.

The lead-time release performance in this example is, at least, going to delay the product schedule by 11 days – based on the "slipping" of the right forging schedule by that number of days. Of course, if the project manager had diagrammed the schedule in a Gant chart format it might become evident that the cumulative effect of the eight items slipped is even more than 11 days.

The data can also be graphed. However, the graph doesn't seem to add much in this case (see Fig. 3.7).

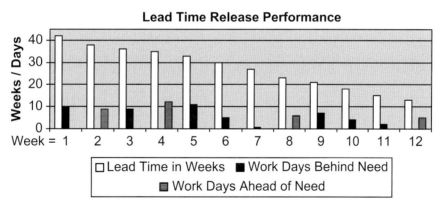

Figure 3.7 • Release in lead-time performance.

It could easily be argued that this is the most important of all release process metrics and should therefore be labeled Gold and perhaps even done daily in some environments.

Release time benchmarks

This analyst has few benchmarks for the time from start to tech release. This time obviously varies considerably depending upon the complexity of the product and how many documents are included in an individual release. Considerable variability has been witnessed – three weeks to four months.

The time from tech release to close is a different story. Regardless of the product complexity, experience says that this time should typically be in the one to three work-day range – if the event "support and process docs completed" is left out of the measurement as was done in our example. If this event is included the goal should be somewhat longer depending upon the complexity of the manufacturing and support processes. It should probably be a separate phase in our workflow and be measured separately.

This short benchmark time/goal is also dependent upon technical release, meaning just that – that the technical issues have been resolved, testing completed as necessary, team review of the document(s) completed, documents signed as required, etc. – as shown in Fig. 3.2.

Support and manufacturing process documents

Support documents would include: assembly and fabrication instructions, quality inspection and testing instructions, field support manuals, even sales literature. Include any of the company technical documents that depend upon the release of design documents for completion.

When new design items are released by Engineering/CM the release document should specify the support documents required to follow. Time lapse from tech release to completion of each should be measured in an ideal world:

- Manufacturing processing instructions
- Quality assurance instructions
- Packaging docs/instructions
- Product manuals
- Package artwork.

At the very least, the time to completion of the packaging and technical publications should be measured. If this is not being done the CM manager should do it. Why? Many companies have designed, ordered parts, built and tested the product only to have it reach the shipping dock and be lacking packaging materials and instructions. The publications have the same issue – often not available to ship with the first product and more often not up to date.

The package art is listed separately in order to emphasize its importance and to note the fact that it should be under documentation control, tracked and released – even though it is sometimes a Marketing responsibility.

Other engineering release metrics

Many other metrics might be added to the CM/Engineering arena:

- Quantity of new specs, assemblies, modules released/not yet released
- Lines of software code released/not released

- Engineering hours per new drawing, spec, etc.
- Design-drafting hours per new drawing, spec, etc. (a NASA employee reported in a seminar that the average assembly drawing took 30 hours of preparation time)
- Time to obtain approvals/number of signatures, by department, by type of release, etc.
- CM and checking hours per new doc.

Some of these elements might be added to the lead-time tracking as per Table 3.5. Some might merit separate charts or graphs. Some may already have been prepared by folks in the Engineering organization. The time to obtain signatures on the release document (ECO or whatever) and the number of signatures on the documents themselves is often excessive and should be measured separately.

In many companies the drafting lapsed time is excessive and should be measured separately (see Fig. 3.8).

In this case the lapsed time seems excessive. This may be due to an excessive backlog. It might also be due to the Design-Drafting Department obtaining too many signatures on the new documents. Without including time for obtaining signatures, an average of seven work days lapsed time should normally be obtainable (see the *EDC Handbook* for ideas on lapsed time reduction).

Release process quality

How will we know if the process improvements in speed or efficiency are improving or diminishing the quality of the release process? What if we improve the speed, and the quality of the product is worse? What if we increased or decreased the number of signers? What if we meet face to face vs. "online"? What if we

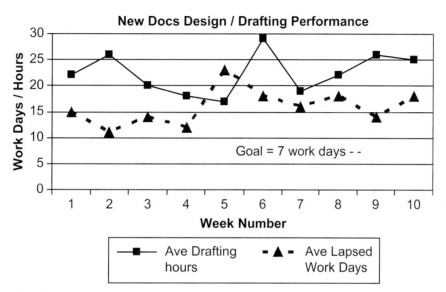

Figure 3.8 • Design-drafting time performance.

change drafting standards? What if we revise the release form? What if we change the event sequencing in the process? Don't we need an objective measure of process quality?

Recognize that our product is documentation. Therefore we need a method of determining whether the quality of the documentation is improving over time. Consider then, the use of the number of changes to the new released documents/software module as a fair indicator of the quality of the process – much as was done in Table 3.2. This will, of course, require discipline in the application of one problem: one fix, one change action, as will be discussed later. Track the documents released each week by part number. Track the revisions to each in the next six months and calculate the average number of changes per document (see Table 3.6).

If the quality of the process is improving, we should see a decrease in the average revisions per document. In this case, something has changed to degrade the process. If we graph the results, that picture may better point to the approximate time the degradation began (see Fig. 3.9).

It is obvious that something occurred about week 3 or 4 that began a degradation of the process quality. The revisions per document increased significantly, then decreased, but not to the original level – let alone showed improvement. One company found a similar condition and realized that they had changed to online review and sign-off at that time. They returned to face-to-face review and approval meetings and returned to a more acceptable level of doc revisions.

This writer believes that with most real process improvements, the quality of the process will also improve – but we need to measure it to be sure.

Release phase status

Most companies have, consciously or unconsciously, phases in the new product development lifecycle. They are more or less documented. Often the chief engineer writes a very detailed document about the engineering steps that should normally be followed in new product development. However, there is often a failure to tie this detail to a broader company scope. There is often a failure to tie that development process to the documentation and bill of material (BOM) that the rest of the company uses.

Table 3.6 Release process quality data

GOLD		
Number of docs released this week	**Revs to docs in the first 6 months**	**Ave. revs per doc**
27	35	1.3
21	39	1.9
30	44	1.5
19	39	2.1
5	17	3.4
14	38	2.7
25	56	2.2
21	46	2.2
16	39	2.4
15	38	2.5

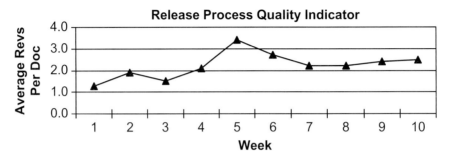

Figure 3.9 • Release process quality indicator.

Company-wide phases need to be defined in terms of BOM status and drawing status. One should be able to look at the system(s) and the documents and tell which phase they are "valid for." We should not want to put a product into production which has parts, specifications or assemblies that are only valid for pilot production, for example. We should also not allow parts to be purchased for production that are only valid for pilot – or parts to be purchased for pilot that are only valid for development.

Of course, the number of phases and the terminology varies significantly from company to company. Those doing military work tend to use the Department of Defense (DOD) terminology while the commercial market varies considerably.

Some companies try to do without a particular phase – most frequently the pilot phase. This is normally a significant mistake, as is pointed out in more detail in the *EDC Handbook*.

Many of the metrics outlined in this work should be done for both pilot and production. Every company should have this or a similar method of tying the phases to the system and the documentation. Every company should have this kind of block diagram, Figure 3.10 showing one logical methodology and terminology, somewhere in their standards.

This method uses the document revision level (date, numeric, alpha) as a technique for indicating which phase an item is valid for. Then a corresponding system code is assigned (ESP). This is done so that anyone can look at either the document or the system and see what phase an item is valid for – and they must agree.

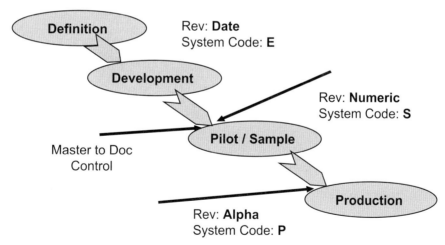

Figure 3.10 • Product/document/item/BOM release phases tied together.

Such a block diagram also helps tie together the release process with the change, BOM and order entry processes.

Benchmarking survey – release process

For comparison the applicable portion of the benchmarking survey is as follows:

Products released per year:
"New" 40 average, range 0–600
"Spin-off" 112 average, range 0–250.
Comment: "New product" is a subjective term. Many may call a product "new" while you or I might say "spin-off" or vice versa.

Part numbers assigned per week: 26 average.

Form used:
Yes 64%
No 36%.

Signatures on the part number assignment form:
29%, 0 or none
53%, 2.7 average, range 0–15
18%, no answer.

Comment: Range 0–15, some must have meant PNs assigned, not signatures. Why would anyone have to sign a PN assignment action?

Part/doc number/rev. level maintained in:
Hand-kept file 17%
Database 40%
Both 43%.
Comment: Get rid of those old hand-kept card files.

Document number is:
Embedded in the PN 77%
Separate/cross-referenced to the PN 23%.

Comment: To the 23% – if you ever change your PN system, go embedded with a tab.

Significance in part numbers (see Fig. 3.11):
Significant 24%
Non-significant 17%
Semi-significant 59%.
Comment: Always tab/dash – other significance is sometimes good, sometimes not. See the author's website for an article on PN significance.

To find similar items – Use a separate class code/group technology code cross-referenced to the PN:
Yes 66%
No 34%.

Significance in Part Numbers

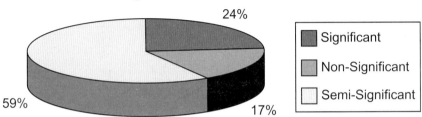

Figure 3.11 • Significance in part numbers.

Have a "smart title/description" that allows word search to find similar items:
  Yes 60%
  No 40%.

Tabulation "ability" in the part number (see Fig. 3.12):
  Tab PN 68%
  No tab 32%.
Comment: To the 32% – at the first opportunity look at adding a tab to every number. Tabs will be for tabulated documents, non-interchangeable change; some may never be used but you will have one if needed and you will be consistent.

Product design docs released per week (exclude new docs in changes): 27.5 average, range 2–500.

Tabulate the Part Number

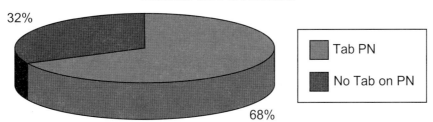

Figure 3.12 • Tabulation "ability" in the part number.

Form used:
Yes 82%
No 18%.

Number of signatures required on release doc: 4.2 average.

Release phases:
Quote/definition 36%
Design/development 79%
Pilot 46%
Production 88%.

Generally, release is done:
An item at a time 49%

An assembly at a time 40%

A product at a time 39%.

Comment: Some companies obviously allow more than one or allow all methods.

The release phase is identifiable on docs by:

Design/development _____ (e.g. date)

Pilot _____ (e.g. numeric rev.)

Production _____ (e.g. alpha rev.).

12 no answer

9 can't tell any

19 can tell all

18 can tell some but not all phases.

Comment: Shouldn't one be able to look at a document and tell what phase it is valid for?

A team (concurrent engineering, design, cross-functional, etc.) meets frequently during design and development:

Yes 63%

No 37%.

Opinion – Team functions well in our company:

Yes 54%

No 8%

NA 38%.

Opinion – Team has reduced the number of changes required:
Yes 35%
No 27%
NA 38%.

The manufacturing process requires:
Assembly drawings to be used on the production floor 76%
An assembly process is written and has "mini drawings" 33%
Assembly drawings and assembly process on the floor 53%
Photos/video/models are used on the floor 19%
Other assembly doc method 9%
Fabrication process/routing use the part drawing 23% (see comment)
Other fabrication doc method 12%.

Comment: Many companies do not do their own part fabrication, thus only about a third answered the fab doc question.

Chapter Four

Order entry and fulfillment

All product manufacturing companies have a sales/marketing function, take orders, process orders, design and build as required, and fulfill those orders. All product manufacturing can also be divided into some basic types:

- **Design to order** – may or may not include a pilot product build.
- **Make to order** – some unique design is implied.
- **Make to stock** – implies that product is typically in finished goods stock awaiting shipment.
- **Make to print** – fabrication of parts or assemblies to the customer's specifications.

Many companies do two or more of these types of business. Each has its unique problems/challenges and each requires some differences in its metrics. Almost all, however, have an order entry function and follow the same general order fulfillment process.

Order entry process

The functions performed in the order entry process are sometimes ignored by the management. An order comes into the plant, it is celebrated and seemingly forgotten. The Order Entry Department should have policy and procedure for tracking the order to fulfillment – this is not normally a function of CM concern. However, if metrics are not available, CM should undertake those, if/as time is available, especially if Design Engineering is involved.

There are some key points/dates that should be measured to follow every order to completion/fulfillment and to set the stage for improving that process, especially improving the "turnaround time":

- Customer gives the order to Sales/Marketing/Configurator Module System.
- Order is forwarded to Order Entry.
- Order Entry enters the order into the MRP/ERP/Configurator Module System.
- Design effort, if required, is completed.
- Order is scheduled.
- Build is completed and sent to finished goods stock (FGS).
- Order is shipped to the customer.
- Order is received by the customer.

Order entry is sometimes done online by either the customer or sales. Sometimes the Order Entry System is linked to the MRP/ERP via a Configurator Module or otherwise.

The above steps essentially occur in series. Yes, concurrent engineering teams can and should be functioning throughout the process in order to minimize the time in each step and in total, but each step cannot be completed until the prior step is completed.

This order entry process may have been preceded by some cost estimating, quoting and contracting processes. Depending upon the type of business, some of the above steps may be skipped. For example, a make-to-stock company will seldom involve Engineering in this process because the product has been previously designed, released, built and sent to stock. A design to order may not include a product build. A make-to-print company will typically not require design effort except perhaps to identify differences in prints quoted and prints as ordered.

Some companies choose to consider shipment to the customer as fulfillment since they consider the time to ship to be out of their control. This may a reasonable stance if the method of shipment is designated by the customer in the order/contract document. If the customer hasn't specified the shipment method then the shipping time should be included in the metrics.

Order fulfillment

Every company should track the orders through the above steps, as applicable. The Order Entry function would be the natural place to do this – the process "owner" as some like to say. If that tracking isn't taking place, then the CM function should be given/take the authority to do it. In the "worst case" all eight steps should be tracked. The data would be measured by date, converted into lapsed time and averaged as shown in Table 4.1.

Table 4.1 Order fulfillment time in lapsed days

Order number	Order to OE function (work days)	Order into system (work days)	Design docs released (work days)	Order scheduled (work days)	Build to FGS (work days)	Order shipped to customer (work days)	Order received by customer (work days)	Total order (work days)
1	4	3	9	5	19	3	5	48
2	5	7	11	3	23	2	4	55
3	6	4	14	2	20	4	4	54
4	1	2	16	4	17	1	3	44
5	7	3	0	2	14	3	2	31
6	2	5	4	3	21	2	5	42
Ave.	4.17	4.00	9.00	3.17	19.00	2.50	3.83	45.67

In this example, each of six orders has been date tracked through the entire process and the dates converted to work days according to the fiscal calendar. The data should be kept for all completed orders during the week or month – frequency of reporting probably based upon the volume of orders. A make-to-stock company might even report daily.

These data are fairly self-explanatory. The unique design work and build obviously take the major share of the total time. The "other" functions, although only taking two and a half to four work days each, collectively take almost as much time as Operations does and more time than Engineering. A static picture of the average lapsed time in each function might be a little more revealing – showing the relative magnitude of each department's process time. We can then more easily tell where to concentrate our effort to reduce the overall average time. Let's assume that these six orders were all the orders in one month (see Fig. 4.1). This bar-graph does not show significantly more information than the data table in Table 4.1.

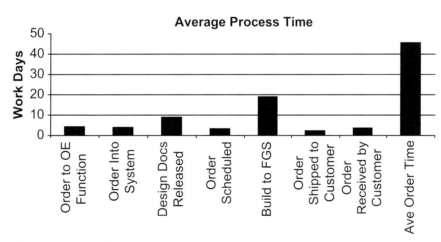

Figure 4.1 • Average order processing time.

If it is believed that any part or all parts of the process are taking an excessive amount of time, the bar-graph may well be called Silver or Gold. For example, in one electronics company, it was believed that since all the parts for build were on hand, the manufacturing build time was excessive. They measured the lapsed time to build separately and assigned a team to reduce the time to a goal of ten work days. It took about five months but was successful.

The data should be collected for every function separately and reported frequently, certainly no less often than monthly. Every function should have a thru-put time report showing their individual performance – or perhaps the CM function should do them all. These reports should probably take the form of a simple graph – work days vs. the unit of time. The result would be eight graphs plus a graph to show the *total* order fulfillment time – the total graph as shown in Fig. 4.2.

Most companies have some "dead time" in the order fulfillment process. There are delays, dwells, queues that often far exceed the "hands on" processing time. Most should have a goal for time reduction. In this case, the goal was set by the executive management – reach 30 days average in 13 months – quite arbitrarily. An improvement team was put in place and did their job very well, although the company in this example only reached the 33–35 work day range. That was still better than their competition. They took about a day off most steps, about two out of engineering time and about three out of the manufacturing build time.

The volume of orders and the orders in process (WIP) might also be added to each function's graph. Tracking the WIP would especially be beneficial because it gives a forecast of process time potential trends.

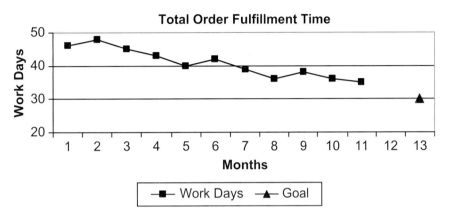

Figure 4.2 • Total order fulfillment time.

Promise to deliver

All too frequently the Marketing folks and others collaborate for an hour or so about the correct promise to deliver time. They give it a WAG (wild *blank* guess) or SWAG (scientific wild *blank* guess), with few data. In all types of manufacturing, Marketing/Sales can and should develop and use the above data for making promises to customers for delivery time/date. They should use the actual average – not the goal or anticipated time. The typical company gives infinitely more effort toward the cost/price than is usually given to the delivery time commitment. Much better that the above measurements be taken and the promises based on fact – what a revelation!

The promises made should also be compared to the actual delivery for each and every order. This is a measurement that is normally made, although often not given the visibility to produce heat and improvement. It can be done by several different methods:

- Percentage on time, percentage late, percentage early
- Work days on time, late, early
- Both.

Measurements would, of course, begin with dates – promised date compared to actual delivery date. That date data would have to be reduced to orders on time, early and late in order to develop the percentage on time, etc. Thus, the measurement data for both metrics would be as shown in Table 4.2.

If we were to consider only the orders on time/late/early we can develop a metric as in Fig. 4.3.

Perhaps a better way of viewing the data would be by percentage of orders (see Fig. 4.4). This graph clearly highlights the problem – far too many orders delivered late. A significant effort is certainly required to correct this problem. An improvement program by an executive, a team, or preferably both, is in order. The ideal, of course, would be for all orders to be on time, not early or late – especially with the emergence of just-in-time (JIT) manufacturing.

Make to order

Typically the make-to-order company or portion of the company business is very much dependent upon their ability to deliver when promised and to outperform the competition in "promise to deliver" time

Table 4.2 On-time delivery performance

GOLD							
Week number	Quantity of orders in the week	Quantity on time	Percentage on time	Quantity late	Percentage late	Quantity early	Percentage early
1	22	2	9.1	18	81.8	2	9.1
2	20	1	5.0	16	80	3	15
3	27	3	11.1	24	88.9	0	0
4	23	4	17.4	17	73.9	2	8.7
5	23	2	8.7	18	78.3	3	13
6	31	6	19.4	21	67.7	4	12.9
7	18	2	11.1	12	66.7	4	22.2
8	35	3	8.6	28	80	4	11.4
9	30	1	3.3	26	86.7	3	10
10	28	7	25.0	16	57.1	5	17.9
11	16	2	12.5	11	68.7	3	18.8
12	26	0	0.0	21	80.8	5	19.2
13	33	4	12.1	23	69.7	6	18.2

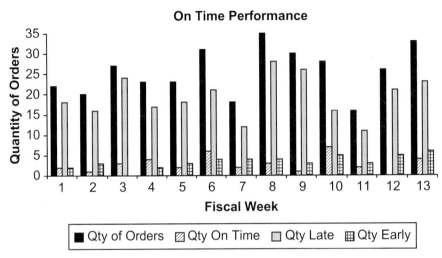

Figure 4.3 • On-time performance by order quantity by week.

performance. If the Front End Loader Company is promising delivery of a featured and optioned product in 24 weeks and the competition is promising 15 weeks, considerable business may be lost to the competition.

Development of new basic products would follow the "time to market" metrics outlined earlier.

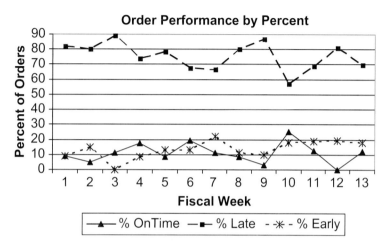

Figure 4.4 • On-time performance by order percentage by week.

Design to order

Metrics would be much the same as referenced in the make-to-order environment. Much more emphasis should be placed on the quality of design – changes required to meet spec, for example.

Make to print

Make-to-print companies have the same metric challenges as make-to-order environments, plus some unique cost estimating and other issues we will not go into here.

Make to stock

Measurement of the order fulfillment time would typically be done in work hours or work days since the items ordered are normally in stock. If the item ordered was not in finished goods stock then the time for that order might include manufacturing build time, test time, etc. and a separate metric prepared.

Development of new products would follow the "time to market" metrics outlined earlier.

Order entry and fulfillment process quality

As viewed by the customer, the time to fulfill an order is an important quality-of-service issue. Some don't mind if the product is delivered early and some do, but almost no one likes a late delivery. Thus, Fig. 4.4 shows a process quality metric as well as a company order performance metric.

There is, however, an even more important quality criterion – the customer must get exactly what they think they ordered. A means of finding out about any failures in this area is needed and should be a Gold metric. If one such circumstance exists, it is one too many. One electronics company didn't wait for customers to tell them about problems. They had the Order Entry staff telephone each customer/order to ensure they received what they thought they had ordered.

Each and every such discrepancy must be carefully followed to the root cause and fixed quickly to prevent re-occurrence.

Chapter Five

5

Bill of material (BOM) process

A bill of material (BOM) is simply defined as a compilation of parts list for a product. A parts list is conversely most simply defined as a single-level BOM. The BOM is typically thought of as a "thing" or a database, rather than a process. This may be one of the reasons why most companies develop more than one BOM/parts list – more than one data entry of the parts lists. This condition is then followed by endless debate over "which is the official BOM," endless reconciliation, endless wasted effort doing multiple data entries of identical data and endless risk of ordering or building the wrong item. Another cause (buy another software program [for whatever reason] and add another data entry) of a strong touch of insanity. A single data entry of the parts list data should be a "no brainer" goal.

BOM process standards

The BOM should be treated as a process, beginning with your standards:

Quantity and Units of Measure – Define the acceptable units of measure and   Yes ☐   No ☐
quantity digits to be used.

Bills of Material – Define the BOM content, structure and policy.   Yes ☐   No ☐

Controlled Engineering Parts List – Defines the elements and format for a parts list   Yes ☐   No ☐
that contains only the design data for an assembly.

Thus, start treating the BOM as a process and measure that process with regard to key elements. The BOM process begins with the assignment of a new part number. Note that there is not a separate BOM flow diagram because the parts list/BOM is created during the release process and changed during the change process, just like any other design document.

Part number assignment

The part number assignment should be a simple process. Any engineer should be able to go to a log and obtain the next part number (PN) giving their name, date, an item description and the product/model it is to be used on – no signatures, approvals or blessings needed. After the PN is assigned the CM folks should put it into the item master file and into the product parts list. Engineering should be encouraged/required to make the document available as soon as possible for review, comment, quoting, etc. Key to this would be to keep revision control solely with the engineer (in development) while the document is made available in the system as part of a preliminary sutructure.

Measurement of this activity by key dates will allow reduction of the dates to lapsed time and would yield the measurement in Table 5.1. The purpose of entering the PN into a preliminary product structure is to show the status of each item in terms of development, pilot, or production. New items would of course be in "development" status. This will allow the team, management and others to view the project status easily. With the part number and document now available in the applicable system(s), the remainder of the departments affected can estimate/calculate and enter their data into the item master file.

Item master file

The item master file is made up of data about the item that originates with each applicable department: Design data (PN, description), Purchasing data (purchased cost, buy lead time, acceptable sources), Manufacturing data (fabrication cost, fabrication lead time, assembly time and hours), Accounting data (standard cost, labor rates, overhead rates), etc. Certain basic part-related engineering data have already been input by CM – the part number, revision level, description, unit of measure, release status code "development," etc.

Once folks know that a new PN has been assigned, and that an "in development" drawing or specification (under Engineering's control) is available, there are two basic methods of populating the item master (IM) file:

1. Each department feed their data to a single function and that function enters the data to the IM file.

2. Each department separately enters their own data.

Table 5.1 Part number and document availability

SILVER		
Part number	**Work days from PN assigned to PN entered into the BOM**	**Work days from entry to preliminary drawing/spec available**
1234501	1	22
1234502	2	18
1234601	1	27
1234701	3	20
1234503	1	16
1234602	1	14
1234702	2	23
1234801	1	22
1234901	1	26
1235001	1	19
1235002	3	18
1234902	1	16
Ave.	1.5	20.1

Either method requires someone to monitor the IM file to assure timely completeness. Most systems have the ability to flag missing data. This analyst would strongly recommend that the CM function be "that someone" to monitor the system as well as input the engineering data. The same would apply to other (multiple) BOM entries should they exist – good sense notwithstanding.

The measurement might best be done by date complete and, if not complete, the number of fields missing. The dates would be compared to the date of new part number entry or the availability of a drawing/specification, whichever is later, and converted to work days (see Table 5.2).

Careful examination of these data shows some difference between departments, but all taking a week or more to complete their task. Looking at the item master data elements one would wonder why any data element would take more than half an hour to estimate and enter. Of course, the estimator and the person doing the data entry are often different people. Still, this analyst would expect that any department should be able to estimate and enter their data completely within three work days.

The CM manager might set a three-work-day goal for all departments and prepare a graphic for each. Let's take a look at how one such graph would appear – Purchasing item master performance. Let's assume that the part numbers listed above are the releases for fiscal week 1 and that we gathered the same data for another five weeks (see Fig. 5.1).

The fact that every department is using more than five work days might call for a Silver urgency rating. Much worse performance would call for Gold and, when within the three-day maximum, Bronze.

As you can see from the graph, the trend of missing data elements and thru-put time is in the wrong direction and certainly nowhere near the goal. The CM manager should encourage Purchasing to buy into the

Table 5.2 Non-engineering item master data

SILVER						
Part number	Manufacturing elements missing	Work days to complete manufacturing data	Purchasing elements missing	Work days to complete purchasing data	Accounting elements missing	Work days to complete accounting data
1234501	1		2		0	5
1234502	0	6	1		1	
1234601	2		0	6	0	5
1234701	0	4	0	8	2	
1234503	0	5	3		3	7
1234602	0	7	3	7	2	
1234702	1		2		0	4
1234801	3		0	9	2	
1234901	0	5	3		0	6
1235001	0	4	2		0	6
1235002	2		0	7	2	
1234902	0	4	3		0	5
Ave.	0.75	5	1.58	7.4	1	5.42

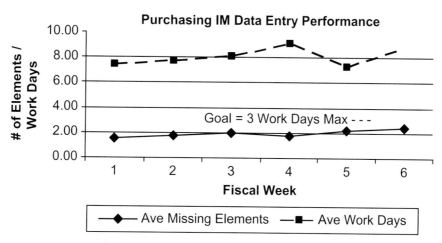

Figure 5.1 • Purchasing item master data entry performance.

goal and to undertake an improvement project. The most often made mistake is to take the time to go to the supplier to get quotes. This will take much longer than having a grizzled IE make an estimate – better also to judge purchased part price variance with a third party cost estimate.

It is critical to get cost and lead-time estimates entered in order to allow the project team to plan the release in lead time and see the product cost developing. Until the IM data entry is done, the engineer and the team are using their own estimates to guide them – better to use the estimates made by the proper people.

It is also important to see the product cost developed earlier rather than later. If corrections need to be made, better to realize that earlier. This is why the BOM should be developed early. The best method is to pick a similar product and delete the items that will be changing and insert the new items. It might also be wise to "flatten" the structure – even to the extent of making the new BOM a single-level structure in the beginning. If the design is entirely new, start it out at a single level – evolve the BOM as described in the *EDC Handbook*. This "flat BOM" approach will allow release without immediately facing the structuring issue. The structure can be agreed upon and done later by CM.

Multiple BOMs

Based on informal polls taken in the author's seminars, about 10% (or fewer) of product manufacturing companies have a single data entry of BOM/PL information. Typically the following BOMs/data entries may be found:

- MRP/ERP input by Manufacturing/Materials/CM
- Potentially another data entry for each plant building the same product
- CAD input by Engineering
- An Excel file input by Engineering in order to put the parts list on the assembly drawing
- PDM/PLM input by Engineering/CM
- Desktop publisher by Publications (partial or complete)
- Assembly instructions input by IE/ME.

The distribution noted in the survey was approximately as shown in Fig. 5.2.

Multiple BOMs / Data Entries

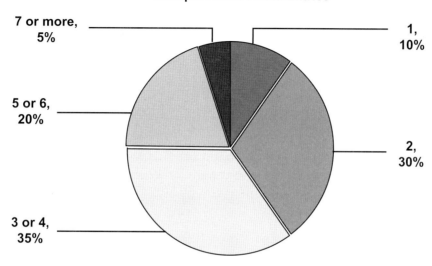

7 or more, 5%

1, 10%

5 or 6, 20%

2, 30%

3 or 4, 35%

Figure 5.2 • Multiple data entries/BOMs.

It goes without saying that companies with more than one data entry of BOM data are practicing some degree of insanity and should formulate plans to attain a single data entry. More than one BOM/view of the BOM is acceptable provided they are all fed by a single data entry. Certainly the first step in such a plan should forbid the purchase of additional data processing programs that would require additional data entry. The plan could be summarized in a time graph but is probably better explained in a text document.

Should the key management not see the wisdom in attaining a single data entry process, the wasted effort to reconcile and correct the various BOMs should be estimated, parts shortages tracked and production downtime estimated.

BOM reconciliation and correction

Certain errors in the BOM should be found by the engineering quality assurance function – Configuration Management. For example, the engineer specified a part and bracket for that part with four holes but only specified three sets of hardware. CM technicians should see this issue and correct it – talking to the engineer if any doubt exists. In another case an error may be made when entering a part number. These design data element issues, when found, should be quickly corrected by an ECO. Corrections should be classified as such on the ECO and counted as such.

If more than one data entry exists, the reconciliation (planned or accidental) will note differences in those databases. If the issue noted is with the design data, correction should be done and counted. If the engineering data elements are incorrect an ECO should be used. If other databases are changed to reflect the correct data, they should be tracked and counted.

Of course the reduction of the number of databases/BOMs (data entries) is the most significant step toward reduction of reconciliation errors.

These corrections and reconciliation actions should be reported to top management in order to shed light on the multiple BOM issue. For a company with many products and several BOMs (data entries) the report might look like that in Fig. 5.3.

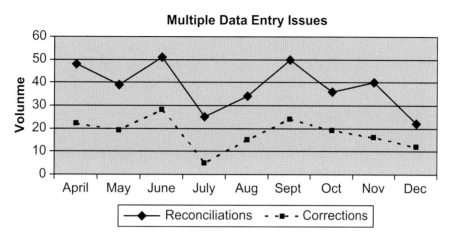

Figure 5.3 • BOM design data corrections and reconciliations.

In this case, the trends of both corrections and reconciliations are positive (downward), although slight. It is fairly obvious that steps need to be taken in the release process toward improved BOM data entry checking. Many companies have multiple checks/signatures on their drawings but zero signatures/checks on the BOM or parts list. One company with a high volume of corrections instituted a process wherein the entry technician printed a copy of the parts list, checked it and signed it. Another CM technician checked and also signed a parts list. In their case the signed parts list was kept in a temporary file and thrown away after six months. However, this step reduced their corrections significantly.

Similar measurements might well be done for other than engineering data – supply chain, production control, accounting, etc. More will be said about BM corrections and measurements when discussing change control quality issues.

New product BOM status

This segment might have been placed in Chapter 3. However, it is also a BOM issue that needs to be in the CM manager's metrics arsenal. As indicated, every company should code the status of an item in the BOM (and on the drawing as well). The Front End Loader Company uses the "ESP" coding convention:

- E = engineering phase
- S = pilot or sample phase
- P = production phase.

Thus, if an item is coded "E" it has not been approved for pilot units. If pilot units are built/planned to be built with any "E" items, it should be made vividly obvious to the management and the team. Likewise if we plan to build a production run with any E or S items, there is a serious validity issue. The CM manager can highlight the issue(s) by examining a BOM for status coding and preparing a graph such as that in Fig. 5.4.

In the above example, the new development project was scheduled to go into pilot *shipments* on week 11. At that time, several items (eight) were still in E code status. This may or may not be a tolerable condition depending upon whether or not it is expected to ship pilot units to internal customers for testing, or it is expected to ship to friendly customers for field testing, or to ship to cash customers.

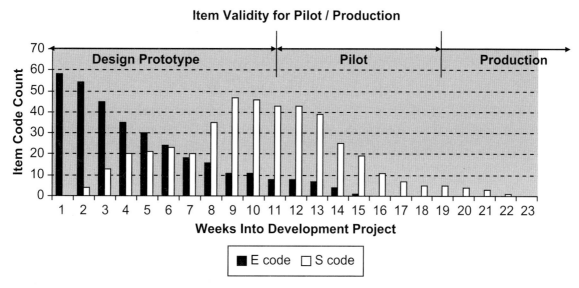

Figure 5.4 • BOM item validity coding.

In week 19 it was expected to begin production *shipments*. Many companies would consider the shipment of units containing pilot status items to be intolerable. Some companies would ship but with a deviation attached to the product and communicated to the customer(s) with a promise to retrofit any items not meeting production standards. A few companies will ignore the situation.

Regardless of the management reaction to the conditions, this metric should be reported to the highest levels of management as well as deviations prepared.

BOM levels

The tendency for companies to create multi-level assembly structures seems to be overwhelming. This analyst has witnessed 11 levels at a couple of companies and had a seminar attendee tell of 16 levels. Many departments wish to add structure for their apparent need and many needs are not in the best interest of the company as a whole. Because agreement cannot be reached on one structure, often an "Engineering BOM" and a "Manufacturing BOM" are created. Often the Materials folks create a "Planning BOM." Many times the various departments can only reach agreement by adding levels to the BOM. Often, such different "views" are achieved by separate data entry.

This analyst believes that fewer levels in a BOM structure result in easier communications and more efficient release, BOM, request and change processes. Three or four levels should be sufficient in almost any

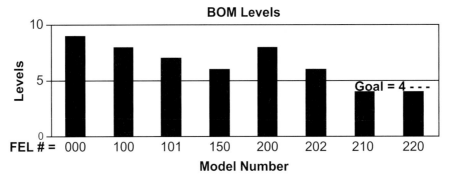

Figure 5.5 ● BOM levels by product model.

company. For a much more complete discussion of BOM structuring, see the *EDC Handbook*. If you subscribe to this judgment, and have too many levels, then setting a goal of say four levels and measuring successive product releases may be in order. Such a measurement might appear as in Fig. 5.5.

At one vehicle manufacturer with nine levels in their first product, they determined that they should normally have four or fewer levels in their assembly structure. Rules were developed as to when a level was acceptable and when not. Over time they achieved their goal but not without glitches and pain. In the end, no one was completely satisfied with the compromise but everyone had to agree that fewer levels made for a more usable, accurate and efficient BOM.

Benchmarking survey – BOM process

For comparison the applicable portion of the benchmarking survey is as follows:

Manufacturing resource planning (MRP) system used:
    Yes 89%
    No 11%.

MRP system name:
    Home grown 16%
    Purchased 84%
    Homegrown 9
    Man–man 7
    AMAPS 3

BPCS 5

MAPICS 3

Remainder 1 or 2 companies each – too numerous to list.

Comment: Survey was taken before BAAN and SAP became popular.

MRP based on:

PC 24%

Mainframe 76%.

Comment: Many more systems PC based today.

MRP code modified (see Fig. 5.6):

A little 41%

A lot 31%

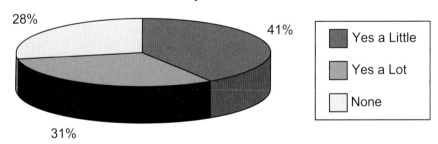

MRP System Modified

28%

41%

31%

- Yes a Little
- Yes a Lot
- None

Figure 5.6 • Modification of MRP code.

None 28%.

Comment: Few, if any, MRP/ERP code modifications should be required. Almost a third of the companies surveyed thought that a lot of modifications were required – much better to change policy and procedures to conform to the system as coded.

Item/part master data entry by EDC/CM:

All 58%

None 23%

Some 19%.

Parts list entry by EDC/CM:

Yes 71%

No 29%.

Typical number of product assembly levels: 4.0 average.

Comment: Two to four is reasonable. This writer has witnessed 11 and heard from seminar attendees of many more.

Who structures the products (see Fig. 5.7)?

Team 52%

Engineering 23%

Manufacturing Engineering 11%

PC/Materials 8%

CM 4%

Product Structure Determined By:

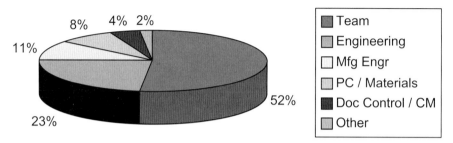

Figure 5.7 • Product structure determination.

Other 2%.

Comment: There should be a single product structure agreed upon by the team.

Number of parts in a typical product: 353 average, range 3–3700.

Number of products active (now being sold): 1704 average, range 3–46,000.
Comment: Some of the answers may be "products structured" not just "now being sold."

Number of part numbers in the MRP item master/part master file: 49,900 average, range 2000–900,000.

Number of part numbers active (used in products being sold): 24,210 average, range 600–260,000.

Average number of items on a parts list: 30 average, range 5–300.

What is typically on your parts list/BOM (besides parts and components):

Design specs 31%

Packaging (box) material 27%

Product labels 66%

Package labels 36%

Publications 29%

Sales literature 10%

Fixtures/tools 14%

Test equipment 7%

Inspection process 12%

Test process 16%

Assembly process 29%

Test specification 26%

Fabrication process 18%

Process consumable 17%

Other: cross-reference drawing number, customer specs, assembly/fabrication sequencing.

Comment: The manufacturing process should contain process-related items, not the design BOM.

Structure two part numbers in order to purchase an item from two vendors (example: buy an untreated part from vendor A and send to vendor B for heat treatment):

Yes 61%

No 39%.

Structure a part number for every cost center:
   Yes 23%
   No 77%.
Comment: To the 23% – a very questionable practice.

Structure an assembly whenever manufacturing asks:
   Yes 25%
   No 16%
   Sometimes 59%.
Comment: To the 25% – very questionable practice.

Structure an assembly whenever field service asks:
   Yes 7%
   No 27%
   Sometimes 43%
   NA 23%.

The parts list data is hand/key entered to the following databases:
CAD
Structure tree drawing
MRP
MRP at several (___qty) plants
Assembly drawing

Process/routing
Pubs
Other ____qty.

Comment: Question poorly stated. Some interpreted as "done by Doc Control" and some interpreted as "done by the entire company" (as intended). Informal seminar polls indicate that a few have one, some five or six, with an average of about three database entries.

Was a conscious decision made as to items that will be service parts/spares (see Fig. 5.8):

NA 25%

Yes 52%

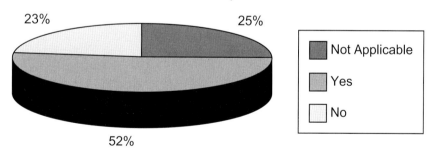

Figure 5.8 • Conscious decision as to service parts/spares?

No 23%.

Comment: "Not applicable" was defined as inseparable or "throwaway" products.

Use of just-in-time manufacturing (see Fig. 5.9):

Some products 44%

All products 7%

No products 49%.

Comment: JIT should require very few levels in the BOM and less debate to agree on one BOM structure.

Typical feature and option count per product (count – not combinations; example: gas or electric start, three color choices, six light packages = 11): 22 average, range 1–208.

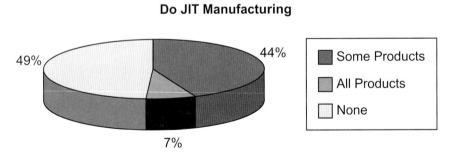

Do JIT Manufacturing

49%   44%

■ Some Products

■ All Products

□ None

7%

Figure 5.9 • Use of just-in-time manufacturing.

Chapter Six

Request process

The request process may refer to a request for design change, drawing/specification change, bill of material change or engineering design action of any sort. This author prefers that the process include all requests for Engineering action. The most important factor in this process is that it must not get intermingled with the change process – as it often does in most companies. Thus, one cannot tell where the request process ends and the change process begins.

The request process should be a simple matter of engineering management accepting responsibility for the issue raised *or rejecting same*. That is, where does ownership of the issue lie? Too often the request is "in limbo" with no clear ownership. The requester thinks that Engineering has accepted responsibility but Engineering merely has it in a queue in the front end of the change process, or worse yet, is blindly proceeding as if every request merits a change. Too often the process treats every issue as a legitimate one and pushes the request into the front end of the change process, often without Engineering actually taking ownership of it.

Sometimes it is left up to each individual engineer to make a decision as to the acceptability/worthiness of each request. All issues/problems/suggestions/ideas are not worthy of a change. Is the individual engineer the correct person to sort out good from bad and to set priorities? Engineering does not have unlimited manpower. Many so-called "cost reductions" (reduce/improve assembly time, repair time, fabrication time, etc.) are not cost reductions if a reasonable payback time is required. The marketplace does not require improvement of some products. Then there is the "lost opportunity" – there may well be a more worthwhile place for the Engineering effort to be spent.

For all the above reasons, a high-level management team should review requests and assure that policy is established in keeping with the resources available.

Request process standards

Thoughtful process design is needed (as well as thoughtful policy, standards, form and form instruction) and a separate flow diagram should be made for the request process. The best of the best practices would have the following standards available:

Request Policy – Outlines the company policy about requests for engineering action.　　　　　　Yes ☐　　　　No ☐

Request Form　　　　　　Yes ☐　　　　No ☐

Form Instruction – Box-by-box instruction for the content required. Electronic forms may have a "cursor pop-up" feature for instructions.   Yes ☐   No ☐

Request Process Flow Diagram/Procedure – Specifies the steps to be taken to process a request and the responsible function.   Yes ☐   No ☐

Teams in the Request Process – Delineate specifics about the team members, chair, meeting time, action items list, etc.   Yes ☐   No ☐

Request flow diagram

The request process can be flow diagrammed rather simply – because it should be a simple process (see Fig. 6.1).

CM is (should be) owner of the process and accompanying policy, form, form instruction and standards. CM should also monitor the process, expedite and measure it. As you can see by the flow diagram, the requests are sent by "anyone" to CM and CM finally notifies them as to the acceptance or rejection. The request itself need only be a statement of the issue with the requester's name and phone number. Smaller companies often do not have a form, only a phone call or note to CM and the list that follows. CM should chair the team meeting and keep the status of the list of open requests.

Request action items list

If no other element of the request process exists, the action items list should be kept. If no request process exists, this measurement/report/log should be the first step in establishing a process. If issues are added by

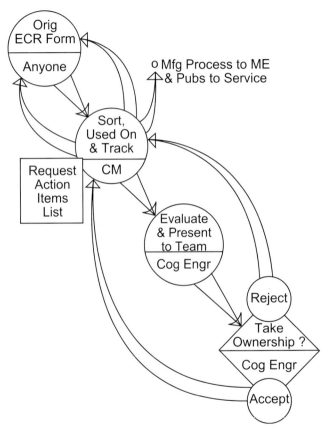

Figure 6.1 ● Engineering request process flow diagram.

phone or email to CM, that would be a good start. This log/report will form the basis for request process measurements.

Some companies refer to this process as an engineering action request (EAR). This name may be even more appropriate than engineering change request (ECR) because it gets the word "change" out of the name. All ideas/issues are not good ones and the major purpose of a request process is to allow sorting of the necessary from the unnecessary.

CM would define the problem with the requestor and the responsible engineer if necessary to present it to the team. The team should ideally be the Chief Engineer, Chief Operating Officer and Supply Chain Chief or their direct representatives. They are in the best position to weigh the issues against policy and manpower. Certain routine requests (BOM corrections/reconciliations and document only changes, for example) need not go to the team (see the *EDC Handbook* for further discussion of the process).

All requests need not go to the team but all should be placed on the action items list and tracked by that report (see Fig. 6.2 for a sample of the report headings). Notice that the report carries the key

ECR #	Request Title	Start Date	Date to CM	Date to Team	Action Required	Action Person	Action Completion Promise / Actual Date	Accept / Reject / Disposition Date	Date Requestor Notified

Figure 6.2 • Engineering request action items list.

dates from the process flow. This measurement/report will allow us to develop other metrics as needed.

ECR or request "titles" should be short but descriptive. If no ECR form is used, the requestor's name and phone number should be added. The team will sometimes have action items to assign to CM, the requestor's management, the Engineering management, the cognizant engineer, etc. These people would be required to give the CM manager promises for satisfaction of those action items. All promise dates, changes thereto and the actual satisfaction date should probably be kept.

The list of requests should include dates of all key the events in this process. Action item dates need not be included since all requests do not have an associated action item and those dates may change. The list would also contain the disposition of the request and date as well as the date the requestor was notified. A record of dates would result that is similar to those in Table 6.1.

This measurement is for example purposes. It contains only those requests that were completed (CM notifies requestor) in a given six-day week. If we prepare a thru-put time report for the entire process (start to notification of the requestor) we would base the report on completions week by week. If we consult a calendar, we can easily turn these data into work days of thru-put time.

Request process time metrics

Among the many requests, some will be accepted as good and necessary changes. Making the requestor wait too long for a decision is also very unproductive. It is therefore necessary to process all requests promptly. That report might look like that shown in Fig. 6.3.

Table 6.1 Extract from engineering change request list

Request number	Start date	Received by CM date	To team date	Team decision to accept/reject	CM notifies requester
123	4/1	4/2	4/9	4/9	4/10
126	3/28	4/2	4/9	4/12	4/12
127	4/3	4/3	4/9	4/9	4/11
129	3/29	4/4	4/9	4/12	4/12
130	4/4	4/6	4/11	4/15	4/15
131	3/29	4/7	4/9	4/12	4/14
132	4/4	1/4	4/9	4/9	4/9
134	4/6	4/8	4/9	4/15	4/15

If needed, a report similar to that in Fig. 6.3 could be prepared for each or any segment of the process:

- Start to received by CM
- Received by CM to team
- Team receipt to team decision to accept or reject
- Team decision to CM notifies requestor.

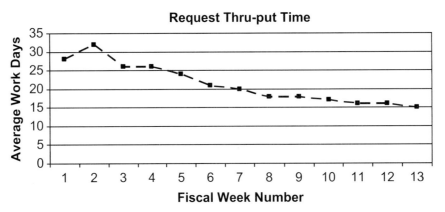

Figure 6.3 • Request process time metric.

Such a report could be done including a WIP count for reference and to aid in the prediction of future process time. This would be an especially good idea if any segment of the process seems to be taking an excessive amount of time. That segment should be singled out for improvement.

When folks establish a request process (or separate it from the change process) and measure it, they are often faced with thru-put times in excess of a month. Average thru-put time of less than a week is attainable. Some companies have achieved three- to five-work-day averages with a totally manual process. It requires the team to meet at least twice a week and it requires careful process design, form design, policy and standards.

Keeping the report on a total time basis is most desirable because all or anyone involved may contribute to delays and queuing of requests in any part of the process. Fast processing also requires training of all

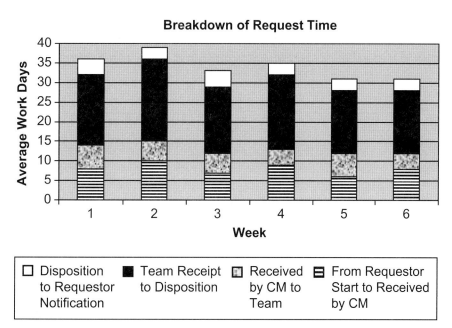

Breakdown of Request Time

Legend:
□ Disposition to Requestor Notification
■ Team Receipt to Disposition
▨ Received by CM to Team
☰ From Requestor Start to Received by CM

Figure 6.4 • Breakdown of the request process time.

involved – even the requestors. The trainer needs to emphasize that the requestor, CM, the team and others who may be consulted are all important to fast turnaround time and a quality result.

A breakdown of the process time into its parts may be a good idea for group training or for the CM manager to use for "one-on-ones" with various folks involved. Such a breakdown is demonstrated in Fig. 6.4.

When training is done, it must include the reasons as to why speed is important. If the issue merits a change, should we take a long time processing it? If it doesn't merit a change, is it productive to leave the requestor "hanging"? See the *EDC Handbook* for much more about the importance of speed in the processes.

Of course it is extremely important that CM lead the way in reducing their process times. At both ends of the process, there is no reason for them to take an average of more than a half-day – one day total. Certainly some requests will require some investigation, but many others will be routine and easy.

This stacked bar graph would not only be an excellent tool to display the total time and the breakdown of that time, but it would also be a good tool to get management attention to an excessive process time problem. It can be used to argue that the team needs to be made up of high-level management who can make policy and priority decisions quicker. This analyst has found that elevating the team membership management level can cut the team process time in half – and cut the meeting time in half.

In one company it was found that the request went from the person who had the issue, to their boss, then to the manufacturing engineer, then to the manufacturing engineering manager and finally to CM. None of these "middlemen" have any responsibility for the design – but they all contributed to the process time. They eliminated the middlemen. That company made sure that they were all notified of the request (via the list) so they could comment to CM or the team if they wished.

As the team operates over time, they will develop criteria wherein the CM manager is allowed to reject certain changes or to bypass the team and go straight to the change process on certain other requests.

Request rejection is OK

Product manufacturing is not a politically correct business. The harsh realities of competition usually preclude acceptance of all requests. This analyst has often noted that the way to tell if the request process is working well is to go out and interview a few people – one each from Purchasing, Manufacturing Engineering, Receiving, Assembly, Quality, etc. Ask them if they have asked engineering to make a document or design change. If they say no, move on. If they say yes, ask if they have learned of the disposition on a timely basis. The answer is often unprintable. It is better in this writer's view to reject promptly than to allow an issue to fester. The requestor always has recourse through their management chain.

Keeping track of the WIP and rejection volume should also be a useful management tool. A report similar to that in Fig. 6.5 is therefore suggested. From the data plotted in the figure, it appears that the rejections are declining and the WIP increasing. This certainly isn't a healthy trend. It likely means that the process time will be increasing and requestors are increasingly frustrated. It is probably an indication that there isn't sufficient engineering manpower to process all the requests, let alone promptly. The team needs to screen the incoming requests much more critically unless additional manpower is to be added.

Of course, this situation isn't necessarily as simple as choosing between rejecting requests or adding manpower. Process improvements might solve the increasing WIP/process time issue. Examination of the reasons for requests and changes might indicate a high number of "corrections," which might indicate work is needed on drafting standards, document checking, check lists, etc. In any event, such a graph allows the management to see the growing problem in perspective.

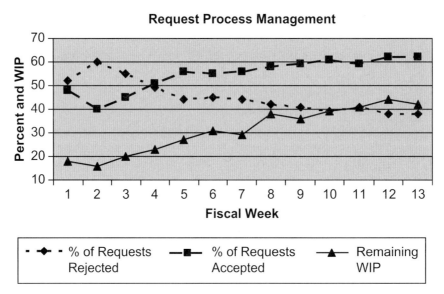

Figure 6.5 • Effective team management tool for the request process.

Those companies that do not have a separate ECR process should examine their change process to see how many changes are in that process that Engineering has not actually taken ownership of. And also, examine the changes passing through the change process that weren't needed or were intended to be cost reductions but aren't. As you will see in Chapter 8, proper screening of requests can result in "new-found" engineering manpower.

Benchmarking survey – request process

For comparison the applicable portion of the benchmarking survey is as follows:

Who can request a design change:
  Any company employee 94%
  Only certain people 6% – engineers, tech function reps, managers.
Comment: Six companies indicated that they had no formal request process. Many people feel that if the ECO process says "anyone can request a change" that such a statement means they have a request process. This is not realistic. Answers are skewed per those responses.

Number of requests per month: 55 average, range 5–300.

Number of people who sign the request before the right engineer sees it: 2.4 average.
Comment: Before the engineer sees it! What value do they add to the process?

Total signatures on a typical request form: 3.5 average.
Comment: Requestor and CM signatures (indicating that it meets the management team's approval) are enough.

Is requestor given an "accept/reject" response (see Fig. 6.6)**?**
  Notified 79%
  Not notified 21%.
Comment: Twenty-one percent of the requestors are kept in the dark – treated like mushrooms. Unacceptable!

Is the Request Loop Closed?

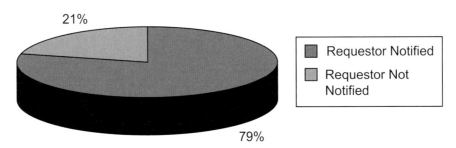

Figure 6.6 • Is requestor given an "accept/reject" response?

Quantity of requests in process: 75 average.

Comment: 75 requests in process divided by 55 average requests per month = 1.36 months. Thus the average thru-put time is almost six weeks – unacceptable!

Is lapsed time measured from "requestor" to "accept/reject" response to requestor:

Yes 38%

No 62%.

Comment: Survey question should have explored the "No" answer further.

Average request to response time: 14.7 work days.

Comment: This is three weeks. Why the apparent discrepancy? That is, the queue calculation above indicates six weeks and answers to this question indicate three weeks. Probable reason: those who don't measure their process time think it is much faster than it really is.

Requests funneled through EDC/CM:
  Yes 80%
  No 20%.
Comment: Is anyone tracking the response time in 20% of the companies?

It is clear as to who the responsible/cognizant engineer is:
  Yes 56%
  No 11%
  Sometimes 33%.
Comment: As you will see below, the "yes" probably includes managers who funnel the changes to their
  people.

Are requests funneled through an engineering manager or other party (not EDC/CM) and then disbursed to a design engineer:
  Yes 40%
  No 60%.
Comment: Engineering managers, project engineers, etc. tend to be a bottleneck and lengthen the
  process.

Chapter Seven

7

Ancillary processes

There are certain company processes that are normally not directly in the CM realm. Such processes have a direct bearing on the success of the CM major processes. These auxiliary processes and the reason(s) why they are so important to best in class CM are:

- **Deviation process** – often misused for making fast changes and temporary changes.
- **Service parts process** – process not delineated and thus all parts and assemblies are thought by customers to be "spared" and they are unhappy with the order fulfillment time.
- **Publications process** – often not ready to ship with the product and/or not up to date.
- **Failure reporting process** – data not fed back to Design Engineering on a timely basis.

Thus, the need for key metrics to be presented for these ancillary processes will be discussed.

Deviations

Deviation, waiver, off-spec, variance and concession are all words for the same beast. Deviations are (or should be) temporary departures from a specified item design for a specific number of units or a specific timeframe. Thus the current design is OK – no need for a design change. Deviations are present in most product manufacturing companies whether desirable or not and whether used properly or misused.

A few companies refuse to have such a process. Those few insist that the product be made exactly as documented – including one the author worked for. If the design will not be changed by engineering, then any deviant items must be reworked, scrapped or returned to the supplier. Such "hard-nosed" management is all too rare but is best practice in this analyst's opinion – as it results in the best of the best product quality.

If a company is to have a deviation process, it should be carefully documented. The following conditions should be outlawed:

1. During analysis of non-conforming material (deviation to the specifications), Engineering agrees to a change in the specification. The material is approved for "use as is" by virtue of the deviation. The engineering change happens weeks or months later or perhaps not at all. The same deviation is often repeated again and again.
2. The fabricator asks for a deviation to the specification for material produced or about to be produced. The material is pre-approved for "use as is" by virtue of the deviation. The engineering

change happens weeks or months later or perhaps not at all. The same deviation may be repeated again and again.

3. The Engineering and Operations folks see the deviation as being a quick way to accomplish a change. The "formal" change is to follow – some day – maybe.

If future failures of the deviated items occur, the engineer performing the troubleshooting is unaware of the fact that the specific item(s) under examination may have been affected. This is simply an intolerable condition. The design change should come first and then the non-conforming material disposition can be "use as is" by authority of the design change with no deviation needed.

In the first two conditions, use of the non-conforming material should not be allowed until the design change is processed, approved and released. This keeps the pressure on the engineer and the engineering change process for quick processing and avoids the need for a deviation.

The third condition is a certain indicator that the formal change process is slow and painful and the folks involved see the deviation as a quick way to make a "floor change". The change process needs work, but chances are that as long as this fast method is available the change process will not get the streamlining it obviously needs.

Most companies allow deviations (good or bad) to be processed without ever posting the deviation in the affected document revision block. Thus the actual configuration of the items affected is lost and future failure troubleshooting is severely handicapped.

Deviation standards

The deviation process should consist of the following (see the *EDC Handbook* for further details):

Deviation Policy – Defines the circumstances wherein a deviation from   Yes ☐   No ☐
existing design criteria is acceptable and for posting deviations into
the document revision block.

Deviation Form – With a box identifying the person responsible for   Yes ☐   No ☐
clearing the deviation.

Form Instruction – Box-by-box instruction for the content required.   Yes ☐   No ☐
Electronic forms may have a "cursor pop-up" feature for
instructions.

Team Standard – Specific membership, signatures, for the non-con-   Yes ☐   No ☐
forming/deviation team to meet daily, etc.

Note that each deviation needs to be posted on the applicable design document revision block. This is a necessity for future troubleshooting purposes. This takes us to the first probable metric (see Fig. 7.1).

The company used as a model for the above was a fairly large corporation with a broad product line. The posting of all deviations to the affected document revision blocks was set as a goal to be achieved in one year or less. It can be seen that the goal was met – but only after considerable resistance. It

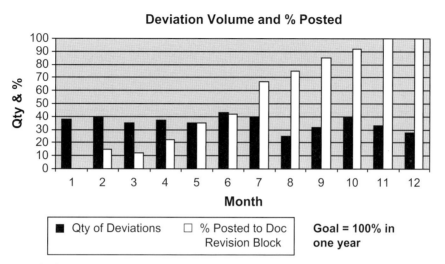

Deviation Volume and % Posted

Legend:
- ■ Qty of Deviations
- □ % Posted to Doc Revision Block

Goal = 100% in one year

Figure 7.1 • Progress to goal of posting all deviations on docs affected.

required considerable training and follow-up with the non-conforming/deviation team to accomplish the goal.

In a smaller company, the goal was set, and training accomplished and met in less than two months. In both companies the prior history of unposted deviations was treated separately and addressed by CM on a blanket ECO basis.

Deviation to make a fast change

Both companies referenced still had many deviations, which were used as a means to do a fast design change. It took a policy change and more training to require the design change to be processed before the material disposition could be designated "use as is." When that was accomplished, about *two-thirds* of the deviations were not needed. The measurement of deviations used as a means of making fast design changes is thus a very important issue. Thus another important metric is needed (see Fig. 7.2).

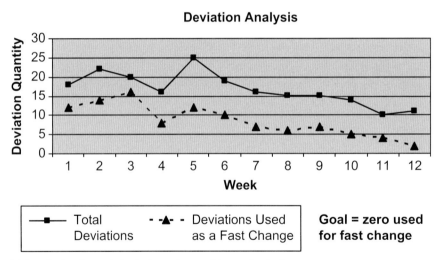

Figure 7.2 • Metric to aid in elimination of deviations for making a fast change.

Of course, both of the above undesirable conditions can be eliminated by the Chief Engineer inserting CM in the deviation *signature* process with instructions not to sign either type of deviation. This is less than ideal but may be necessary. In this analyst's opinion, the best approach is to streamline the change process first and then outlaw these conditions by policy. For this reason, and the progress apparent in the examples, both metrics have been labeled Silver.

Service parts

Some companies mistakenly assume that all parts of the product are for sale and therefore there is no need to identify any parts as "service" or "spares." Investigation will typically show that parts are being taken from the production inventory to satisfy customer orders for service parts. Often an underground service parts inventory exists. The disruption to production schedules and customer commitments for product deliveries is significant.

Further investigation will reveal that Publications has delineated *all* the parts and assemblies in the product. This reinforces the image that all items are not only for sale, but strongly implies that they are available on a quick turnaround basis. Most customers believe that listed items are available in an inventory for their quick service. They are sorely disappointed when some items are rather slow in coming.

Most companies designate certain items as service parts – those subject to wear, damage or frequent failure – and carry a limited quantity of each in a service inventory. This decision is made by the Design Engineer in cooperation with the Service Engineer usually by creating a coded database or documented list. Team review is desirable. The publications then reflect only those items coded/listed as service items.

Typically the result is that about one-fourth of the total part numbers are listed. This saves about three-fourths of the cost of preparing publications exploded views and lists. Does this mean that some items the customer needs will not be furnished? Of course not – the typical method used is to note in the publications that any items not listed will require a quote for price and delivery. With these methods, the production schedule is not interrupted, considerable cost is saved and customers are happy. Every company should therefore have a policy that designates and limits the items designated as service parts.

Service Parts – Defines who and how service parts are chosen and documented.   Yes ☐   No ☐

The Publications organization (sometimes part of Engineering Services) should measure each product's service items as a percentage of the total items. It they do not, CM should measure service items in that fashion. A snapshot of such a measurement is shown in Fig. 7.3. This chart reveals that much progress has been made in the Front End Loader Company but more work needs to be done. It is easy to see the products that need attention. Actually there are three major measurements that might be made in this area. One would determine if a service parts list (or database coding) has been completed. A second would measure the percentage of items spared as in the above figure and a third would measure the Publications reflection of the minimal service items list.

Publications

Publications or service manuals are frequently ignored by management and the CM function. They are extremely important to service people and customers, however. For this reason, some key measurements

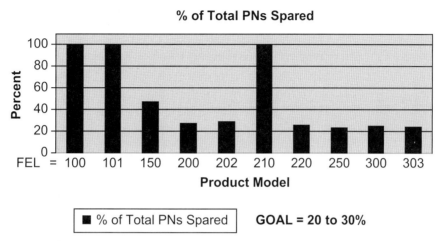

Figure 7.3 • Analysis of service (spared) PNs by product type.

should be made. The service parts discussion above, mentioned one important measurement. There are at least a couple more publications metrics that are critical to customers.

Often the new product publications are not available when the first shipments occur and are frequently not up to date with the product. As unacceptable as it seems, most companies suffer from this touch of insanity. Somehow all the other process and support documents get done, the parts are ordered and made, the parts are shipped, received, inspected, stocked, issued, assembled and the product tested, but the manuals aren't ready or aren't up to date.

- **Negative principle:** R. M. Donovan wrote in *Midrange Enterprise*: "The fact is, most information supplied (to the customer) is excessive, often late and frequently inaccurate."

This writer's experience has been identical. There is no excuse for it, unless management neglect is an excuse. In one company multiple products were being shipped without the publications available and when they were available they were not up to date with the engineering changes. The Quality Assurance folks were examining the pubs for availability and checking to see whether or not they were up to date with the product design. Deviation authorizations (DAs) were written for every product shipped, indicating the discrepancy, but the management weren't aware of or were ignoring the DAs.

Upon analysis, it was quickly revealed that the tech writers weren't part of the team meetings. In fact the pubs were produced by another division of the company on the other side of the city. That division made a different line of products whose pubs were ready when needed and were up to date. When the applicable Publications folks were moved to the division responsible for the product, the issues were fairly quickly resolved and those support documents were up to date and available when the first unit shipped.

This is an extreme example but similar conditions exist in many companies. CM should, preferably in conjunction with QA, produce a metric that tracks pubs' release and update performance. In the case of the company referenced above, it was a simple process of logging data already on the DAs (for a single product measurement see Fig. 7.4).

As the problem was measured and fixed over time, this metric would have started out as Gold and moved finally to Bronze. The solutions for these conditions are not particularly complex. Some of them are:

- Publications people should be part of the CM process teams.
- Service parts need to be identified and limited.

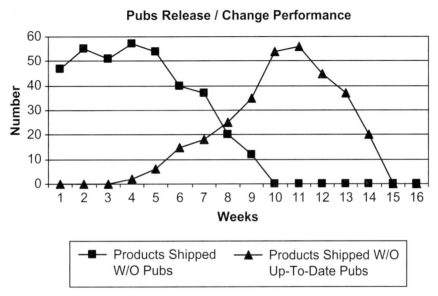

Figure 7.4 • FEL-200 publications performance measurement.

- Publications reflect only the service items.
- Publications initially reflect only the probable top two or three failure modes.
- Technical writers use word conservation.
- Publications are bound such that *page changes* can easily be made – not hard bound.

- Quality Assurance verifies that publications are available with the product shipment and that they are up to date.

In order to achieve such results it is imperative for the company to have a Publications Policy Standard.

Publications Policy – Preparation, content and maintenance of service manuals.   Yes ☐   No ☐

Failure reporting

Product failure information is critical to an engineer's ability to change the product to correct those design issues. It is one of the most difficult processes facing any manufacturing company. The service people are performing their functions at the customer's site or in repair facilities often remote from the factory and from Engineering. When product is returned for repair/refurbishment, the people in that process are often remote from the Engineering function.

Even the operations testing failures (product test, reliability test, etc.) are often not made available to the engineer on a timely basis. For these reasons and others, the failure reporting process needs to be carefully documented:

Failure Reporting Policy – Policies regarding timely and useful reporting.   Yes ☐   No ☐

Failure Form – Information needed on each failure for analysis.   Yes ☐   No ☐

Report Formats – Specify raw data and reduced data format(s).   Yes ☐   No ☐

The policy should set a goal for timely feedback of failure data to Engineering from all points of test/ failure. It would seem reasonable to see this occur weekly with no more than a one week delay. Those data will usually reflect the trial-and-error repair process. Thus when a failure occurs, more than one part or module may be replaced and "no problem found" on some items will result. Such a condition requires analysis. Multiple failures require summation. If data reduction and analysis is occurring, another week or no more than two weeks may be required.

A quandary exists for measurement of failure data. What function should analyze the failure data? Shall we measure the feedback time for the raw data, reduced and summarized data, and/or hold face-to-face meetings to discuss and analyze the failure report(s)? The first step is to determine what information is needed on the individual failure report and to design this "form." Then the time from failure to arrival in Engineering can be measured (see Fig. 7.5).

This is feedback of the raw data, perhaps one report at a time. Service needs to assure that every failure gets reported. Multiple copies may be sent to the Service management as well as to Engineering. If Engineering is responsible for evaluating the failed parts, those should accompany the report. Thus the service, test and reliability functions can each be measured on the basis of individual failure date and the date the individual report arrives in Engineering.

When the data are reduced and summarized, another report could be prepared. The report format might well look like Table 7.1. This report is properly in the sequence of most frequent failures on top, in order to give perspective to the data.

Your report would likely contain considerable other data – customers, sites, date of failure, etc. The service person may have replaced more than one item during repair. If three items are replaced any one, two

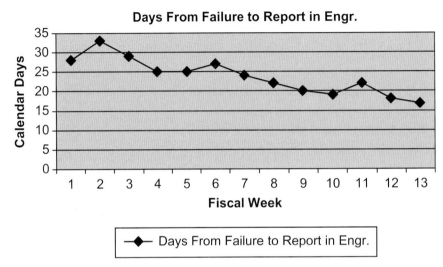

Figure 7.5 • Failure reporting time.

or all three may have failed. Those items will need to be analyzed/tested to find out what probably occurred. The summary report should not wait on the analysis, however.

Other reports by part number, major module, customer, site, etc. might well be produced for the Design Engineer, Quality Engineer or Service Engineer. The overriding factor is the speed with which the data reach the responsible design engineers.

Table 7.1 Sample product failure summary

FEL-303 failure description	PN(s) failed	PNs returned	Known incidents	Last corrective action	Service engineer
Bucket blade teeth broken	768901	768901	127	Replaced	Gregory
Engine timing failure	Unknown	392502 360501	93	360501 replaced	Cross
Track pin/foot	Both	125307 125805	84	Replaced full track	McDonald
Exhaust temp. trips sensor	538703	535805	17	535805 replaced	Venezia
Carb. PCB failure	Unknown	330502 330404 268701	15	330404 replacement	MaDay

Chapter **Eight**

Change cost

So few companies estimate the cost of changes that a university professor, who was attempting to find out what changes actually cost, gave up on the project. This analyst's survey of 58 companies see Chapter 2 about change cost yielded the following:

Benchmarking survey – change cost

Cost of *designing* a fix is estimated on:
  All problems 22%
  Some problems 28%

Few problems 26%
None 24%.

Cost of *implementing* a fix is estimated on:
All problems 17%
Some problems 33%
Few problems 31%
None 16%.

A cost is:
Estimated on a separate detailed form – 19 or 33%
Estimate is summarized on the change form – 21 or 36%
Many answered "yes" to both questions.

Notice that the question wasn't specific as to cost elements included – the CM cost, drafting cost, engineering cost, field fix cost, the unit material or unit labor, etc. Also note that the word "detailed" is subjective. When asked if the participant would furnish a copy of the estimating form, *none responded*. It is therefore probable that total cost and payback are not often done. When the author covers the two-page cost calculation and payback form in seminars (see the *EDC Handbook*) and asks the question "How many of you use a form that is anywhere as detailed as this?" the answer is 0–5% "yes." This also corresponds to consultation experience. Thus this author's conclusion is much like the professor's: few companies calculate the real cost of any changes by any detailed method.

Cost standards

The first critical step in the change cost process is to develop the necessary standards:

Change Cost Policy – Specifies the changes to have cost calculated, estimated,   Yes ☐   No ☐
not required and the company payback period.

Cost Calculating Form – Activity-based cost form with payback.   Yes ☐   No ☐

Cost Form Instruction – Box-by-box form instruction or cursor pop-up   Yes ☐   No ☐
instruction.

This analyst's form is two full pages and closely resembles an IRS form – perhaps this is why so few do detailed cost analysis. The cost process need not be intimidating however, since many changes do not require cost (meet specs, won't fit, etc.) and because few of the form boxes are typically applicable on a given request or change. In practice, the calculation of cost by an ABC (activity-based costing) method is difficult to set up but not difficult to do on any given request or change.

Average cost of a change

The EDC/CM function sometimes calculates a "cost per change." It is normally done to make folks aware that making any change can be costly. These numbers run from $1000 to $4500. Although interesting, such average numbers are generally meaningless. Upon discussion it is obvious that there is a huge difference in what costs are included and aren't included. Generally they include the CM costs, drafting costs and may or may not include any other costs. To be meaningful, the cost of each change (that requires a cost analysis) must be done individually and separately. Such calculation should generally be done to compare design alternatives and to analyze so-called "cost reductions."

Many changes are called cost reductions – including "reduce" labor, reduce time, etc. The cost of making the change must then be balanced against the savings and compared to a company policy on a payback timeframe.

Payback

Most companies have a policy concerning the purchase of capital equipment. They require a saving that pays back the investment in a specified period of time. A machine tool company may require a two-year payback period. A computer company may require a six-month payback. The period depends upon the business dynamics.

The same concept needs to be applied to changes. Every company should have a policy specifying the payback time period for product design changes – perhaps the same as for capital equipment or perhaps not. For example, let's say that the management sets a one-year payback policy. A change that would save X dollars in the first year must then not cost more than X dollars to implement – the one-time or start-up cost.

Either the request team or the change team should be able to request cost analysis. The various departments affected should estimate their time and material. CM should (assuming the manpower is available) gather those numbers and calculate the cost/payback (see the *EDC Handbook* for forms, form instruction and details).

The opportunity for eliminating many requests and limiting changes is significant. One computer company had an 11-person Continuing Engineering function. They were dedicated to improving and cost-reducing production products. A careful cost analysis of the "reduce labor," "reduce assembly time," "reduce maintenance time," etc. with a ten-month payback showed that they had an equivalent of three engineers who were making "cost reductions" that didn't payback as required in new policy – cost reductions that weren't!

Market demand

The same company examined its product line in terms of the market demand for improvement. A high-level management team including marketing folks split the product line into two parts – those products wherein the customers were demanding improvement and those where they weren't. Armed with that information, analysis of changes found that the equivalent of two more engineers were making improvements in products that should not be improved. The result was a windfall of four engineers moved to new product design – one engineer was dedicated to doing cost and payback analysis.

The marketplace may not demand improvement. The company may determine that the product should not be improved because profit will be eroded or a replacement product is in development, etc. Changes to such products are termed by this writer as "creeping elegance" – a gradual way of reducing profit on those products.

Cost metric and application

New products or new start-up companies typically have nearly all changes made to meet product specifications and thus don't require cost analysis. Every mature company or product should analyze changes (or better – the requests) to identify the potential for request denial/change reduction (see Fig. 8.1).

Analysis of Requests / Changes

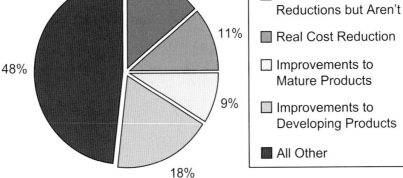

Figure 8.1 • Snapshot of requests or changes.

Making this analysis requires a payback time policy and a division of the product line into "improve" and "don't improve." It can be done for the entire product line or for a single product line. It should be done to aid the request team as a useful tool for rejection of requests.

The cost calculation need not be done on *every* "cost savings" or "time savings" kind of request. The management team can likely estimate the cost/payback without calculation. They (or CM) can certainly reject any "improvements" to products on the "don't improve" list. Publishing such a list will squelch change requests to those products.

Certain requests might be accepted by the request team and still be rejected by the change team after doing a cost calculation. The change team should not proceed if they have doubts about the payback. They should ask CM to gather the costs and calculate the payback, and inform the request management team of the payback analysis.

Such policies and a metric are critical to the reduction of the number of changes and the maintenance of profits.

Real cost reductions

Those changes that reduce product costs within the payback policy requirement are worthy of tracking and some horn-tooting. Such reduction reporting should reflect only the direct material and labor reductions, and only those accepted and implemented that meet the payback policy. The cost reduction tracking will thus not reflect the implementation or start-up cost because real reductions in those areas are unlikely. It must also be realized that the real company cost reduction will not occur until the payback policy period has passed. Thus if the Front End Loader Company has a one-year payback policy, the real reduction in company bottom line will only be reflected one year after each real cost reduction.

Some companies set a goal for real product cost reduction. Care must be taken that material and labor cost estimators are detached from the ownership of the cost reduction goal. If not, it is too easy to attain goals with inflated numbers. Because of possible "estimation inflation," measurement of the product cost reduction should probably be labeled "Silver" rather than "Gold." This is not to erode the meaningful nature of the payback calculation but rather to caution against setting goals for cost reduction. The seemingly simple step of adding cost reduction goals will probably run the risk of number inflation, which can defeat the purpose of payback analysis.

Probably the best metric is to measure and report, product by product, only those changes that have had a payback calculation and without a goal set, as in Fig. 8.2.

Other possible cost metrics

Depending upon the company environment, many other measurements might be taken, not measured in dollars but nevertheless important to the company bottom line:

- Requests claiming savings accepted by the management team without cost calculation
- Requests claiming savings accepted by virtue of acceptable payback analysis (Fig. 8.2)
- Requests claiming savings denied by management team after cost/payback calculation
- Changes denied by change team after cost/payback calculation

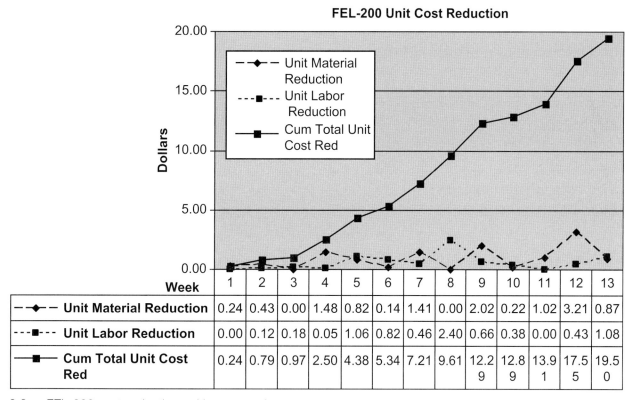

FEL-200 Unit Cost Reduction

Week	1	2	3	4	5	6	7	8	9	10	11	12	13
— ◆ — Unit Material Reduction	0.24	0.43	0.00	1.48	0.82	0.14	1.41	0.00	2.02	0.22	1.02	3.21	0.87
---■--- Unit Labor Reduction	0.00	0.12	0.18	0.05	1.06	0.82	0.46	2.40	0.66	0.38	0.00	0.43	1.08
—■— Cum Total Unit Cost Red	0.24	0.79	0.97	2.50	4.38	5.34	7.21	9.61	12.29	12.89	13.91	17.55	19.50

Figure 8.2 • FEL-200 cost reduction, without a goal set.

- Requests/changes denied by virtue of improve/don't improve list
- Requests/changes accepted by virtue of improve/don't improve list
- Requests not claiming savings and not affecting product on the don't improve list denied by the management team.

Certainly other metrics regarding design, drafting and CM costs may be in order, recognizing that Engineering's primary product is the design document:

- Design hours per new document (average for project)
- Drafting hours per new part drawing, new spec, new assembly drawing
- CM hours per new doc release
- Team hours per new doc release
- Design, drafting, CM hours per deviation, release, request and change.

Bottom line

- **Principle:** If you think cost estimating is expensive, try profit erosion.

Chapter Nine

Change process

Some folks will be surprised to find that we are past the eighth chapter before we get into a discussion of the change process metrics. The change process usually consumes a huge portion of the CM time and management time. One of the reasons for this is that all the issues raised in earlier chapters have not been thought thru, documented, measured and improved as needed. If the processes covered earlier are well-thought-out, documented, measured, and improved and the affected people trained, the change process becomes considerably easier.

That commentary excludes the release process since there will be a strong resistance to releasing any document if the change process is slow and painful. In that sense, discussion of the release process should probably follow the change process. Of course release must occur first in order for product build to occur. It is merely human nature for engineers to resist release when they must look forward to the painfully slow change processes that exist in many companies.

That commentary might also exclude the deviation process because it wouldn't be so readily misused if the change process were fast, accurate, etc.

Measurement and metrics for the change process are critical to the speed, accuracy, communication and improvement of that process. We need to measure the speed, volume, WIP and quality in addition to the cost, as already discussed. We also need to document the process via policy, procedure (flow diagram), form, form instruction and definitions as a basis for training, measurement and improvement.

Discussions in this chapter will presume that some form of request process is in place to limit changes as much as is possible and practical.

Change standards

Documenting the standards not only provides a training method but also a basis for process improvement. The standards that most companies should have in their CM standards manual are:

Change Control Policy – Defines the policy and practices required.   Yes ☐   No ☐

Change Process Flow Diagram (Procedure) – Describes significant process events, the sequencing of those events and the responsible department for each event.   Yes ☐   No ☐

Teams in the Change Process – Best use, membership and responsibilities of the team.   Yes ☐   No ☐

Change Form – Hard copy and/or online   Yes ☐   No ☐

Form Instruction – Requirements for each form box; cursor pop-ups OK.   Yes ☐   No ☐

Interchangeability – Definition and related policy.   Yes ☐   No ☐

Part Number and Revision Level – When to change part numbers and revision   Yes ☐   No ☐
levels, a logic diagram to crisply and clearly define the decisions required.

Change Classification – Defines the acceptable and required change categories.   Yes ☐   No ☐

Mark-Up of Design Documents – Specifies the required methods for precisely   Yes ☐   No ☐
defining the differences between old and new document revision levels.

Effective Point/Date – Defines the points in the manufacturing process and the date   Yes ☐   No ☐
the change will be made effective.

Effectivity Management – Defines who and how effective date (or other) planning   Yes ☐   No ☐
and actual effective change management will be done.

Disposition of Old Parts – Specifies who and how old design parts will be disposed   Yes ☐   No ☐
of, the acceptable categories and who will make these decisions.

It isn't uncommon for a company to have one large epistle that attempts to be an all-encompassing standard of change management. That approach is very questionable. In that case, the CM manager and maybe one other person (perhaps from Quality Assurance) are the only people who have read and understood the entire document. Obtaining approval for issue and change of that document is very difficult because folks are overwhelmed by it. Upon proposing one change to one paragraph or page, the reviewers will bring up issues that have nothing to do with the proposed change. This author's standard for "writing standards" calls for: one subject, one document, normally one to three pages long. Using this "divide and conquer" method will yield easier initial issue approval and easier change approval. This technique also allows for more focused training and process improvement – the most important reasons for writing standards in the first place.

Interchangeability

Probably the single most misunderstood CM issue is that of interchangeability/non-interchangeability. Without clear definition, associated rules and a part number/revision level change logic the change process is subject to stop, hold, delay, argument and some chaos. Thus the single most important metric in the interchangeability arena regards those standards. Are they in place, are they logical and do all affected people understand them? *Yes* or *no*? If the answer is no, take the time to read the chapter on interchangeability in the *EDC Handbook* and to write or rewrite those standards.

Another helpful metric in this area would be to count the changes to each product and the mix of interchangeable/non-interchangeable based upon the age of the product. One might also include with that count the "document only" or "records" changes (interchangeability moot). Thus the entire body of changes can be divided into three categories and measured by a snapshot in time (see Figs 9.1 and 9.2).

Notice that the mature product has and should have a much higher portion of interchangeable changes. The relatively new product would naturally experience a high proportion of non-interchangeable changes. This is typical because any change to meet product specification is, by definition, non-interchangeable and many more such changes occur on new product releases. This is not to say that other changes may not be

FEL-100 Change Type Mix

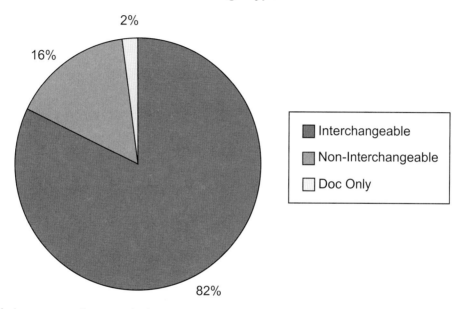

Figure 9.1 • Type of change – mature product.

FEL-210 Change Type Mix

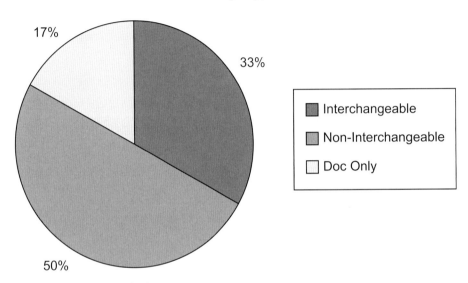

Figure 9.2 ● Type of change – newer product.

non-interchangeable, only that new products typically have a high number of early changes made to meet product spec.

These metrics are labeled Bronze because they must be treated as somewhat vague indicators of problems with product or with interchangeability rules and/or decisions.

Change class

Besides the above interchangeability classification, another helpful method of classifying changes is by "reason" for change – a method every company can benefit from. Careful examination will confirm that all changes will easily "fit" into one or more of these classes:

- Document only change
- Meet product specs (including reliability, maintainability and safety specifications)
- Reduce manufacturing or maintenance cost
- Exceed product specifications (improvements).

Document only changes need to be defined. Include any change that affects the document but not the item delineated – BOM corrections and drawing corrections. The Front End Loader Company also includes changes that make the docs reflect all parts made. Thus if a dimension or tolerance is changed to match *all* parts already made, that change can be included in the document only change category.

Using this classification technique allows good things to happen. The document only change can bypass many procedure flow events. A change required to meet specifications doesn't require a cost calculation. Cost reductions should normally have a cost/payback calculation. Changes to exceed specification should only be done for products on the "improve list." Of course any given change may be done for more than one reason – such as to improve and to reduce costs.

On a given new product, the mix of reasons for change might be tracked as in Fig. 9.3. You will definitely want to access the web link to view this one in color.

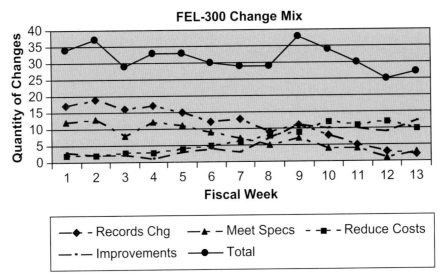

Figure 9.3 • New product changes by reason for change.

This graph is labeled Gold because every product should be measured and reported in this fashion. Management should see the volume of changes by this breakdown and take careful note of the trends. Changes to meet specs should diminish over time, as should records changes. If the product is to be improved, those changes should increase as should real cost reductions, although *both of these reasons have practical limits*. Therefore, over time one would expect the total number of changes to diminish.

Change control process flow

The most critical factor in creation of a fast change process is establishing a flow of events that is logical and compressed. Compression is achieved by putting all the events possible in parallel and in the correct phase of the process. The process can be divided into three major phases with a small but important "point of no return" inserted:

- Engineering or technical phase
- Point of no return/technical release
- CM phase
- Manufacturing or implementation phase.

These major phases are pictured in Fig. 9.4. If your process doesn't "fit" this picture, there are significant issues to address – at least according to this analyst. Those issues must be addressed if the process is to be logical, fast and accurate. However, the process doesn't have to fit this author's definition of logical in order to be measured and to achieve some benefits from measurement. We will use the processes in this chapter, however, for illustration of the change process metrics.

In this process the technical release of the change is accomplished by red-line mark-up of the affected documents. The update of the master docs/CAD will be done in the CM phase. Also in this process the update of the drawings and specs does not wait on the update of the BOM, or vice versa. Many companies insist that the design docs be updated before they update the BOM. That is typically done because the update of design docs takes too long and they are not available when the people using the MRP/ERP system

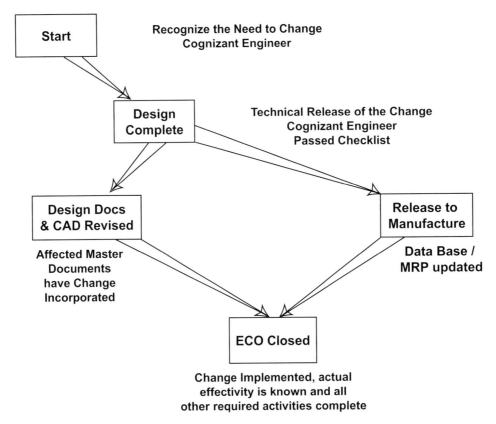

Figure 9.4 • Major process points to measure.

require them. A few companies insist that the BOM be updated before the design docs are. In this process, the update of both is going to happen so fast that the question of sequencing is moot. If you have issues with the change process, consult the *EDC Handbook* for detailed discussion.

Engineering phase

The engineering phase starts with the approval of the change request. If no request process exists or a change isn't required to go thru the request process, the honor system is used to identify the "start" of the process (see Fig. 9.5).

Notice the "clocks" at start and design complete. This signifies the points in this process to be measured. Some or all of the points in between could be measured. If they were all measured it would certainly result in TMI – too much information. If a certain event is especially troublesome, that event might be measured in addition to the total phase.

The review meetings and technical document approval(s) required are obtained in this phase. This is opposed to the typical CCB meeting – Change Control Board meeting – that happens after the engineer carries or sends the change into CM and goes away to work on the next issue. Thus the review meetings are started before the engineer puts fingers to keyboard. At that time they are open to ideas and questions. Technical signature(s) are obtained in those meetings on a marked-up document, again at a point and by a method wherein the engineer is much more open to suggestions.

If customer notification is required, it would take place here. Customer approval, if required, is also started in this phase. If there is doubt of the customer's acceptance, their approval should also be obtained here. If little doubt exists, the team may decide to proceed without approval.

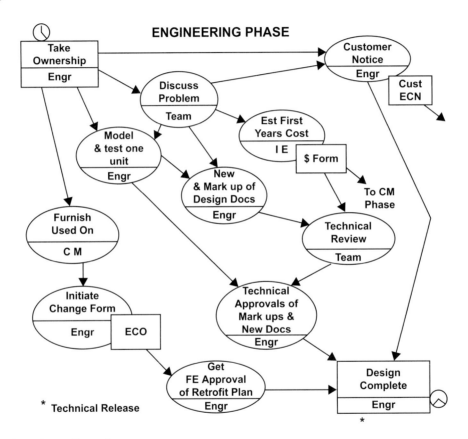

ENGINEERING PHASE

Figure 9.5 • Engineering phase flow diagram.

A similar condition may exist with regard to change cost. If the team requires verification of "cost reductions" the process would be started here – if not ideally done in the request process. If in doubt about payback, hold the change for costing; if in little doubt proceed with risk.

The cost estimate is identified as an IE (Industrial Engineer) responsibility. This might better be a CM responsibility or the responsibility of an IE in the CM group.

Technical release/point of no return

Essentially every process has such a point. It may be too late in the process or too subject to negotiation, however. When the master document has had the change incorporated and the next revision level assigned, the CM function will typically require another change document to be written if further changes or "corrections" are required. Sometimes even this requirement is subject to negotiation. In this process the CM folks will check the documents from the engineer and pass or fail the change at this point – the ideal point of no return (see Fig. 9.6).

The check list should contain only critical items that concern product and design documentation quality.

Examples

1. Are all the affected design documents and design reference documents included?
2. Has the design team reviewed the proposed fix?
3. Are all red lines and/or from–to present and highly readable?
4. Have modeling and testing requirements been met?

CHECK POINT OF NO RETURN

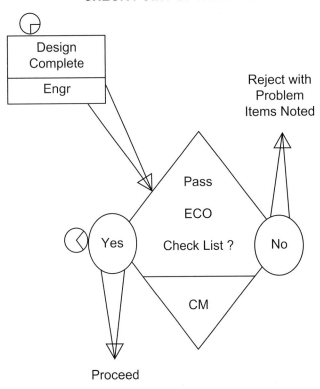

Figure 9.6 ● Point of no return flow.

5. Are any new documents required for the change included and signed?

6. Have the author and acceptor signed the red lines?

Completion of such a check list must occur within one hour of arrival from the engineer. If the check list calls for acceptance, the hour would be charged to CM. If the check list calls for return to the engineer, the hour would be charged to the engineering phase. If your process is excessively long, you may want to start with an initial goal of a half-day allowed instead of an hour.

This analyst sometimes calls this point a "drop dead point." After acceptance, if the engineer emails or walks into CM to stop, hold, or revise the change, he will normally be told to "drop dead." This encourages the engineers to "do it right the first time." It discourages launch of a change without proper modeling, testing, review, approval, etc.

Will there be exceptions to this rule? There are always exceptions – but they must be very rare. The CM manager should be given the authority to allow reasonable exceptions. However, exceptions should rarely be required if the proper policy, procedure, form, form instruction, standards and training are in place.

Having passed the CM check list, the change can now progress into the CM phase.

Configuration Management phase

This phase could be called the technical/administrative phase. The design work and review was complete as demonstrated by signed mark-ups and new documents if required and the check point passed. It is now time to incorporate the change into the masters, plan the effectivity, enter the change into the BOM and notify all affected so they can proceed with their tasks (see Fig. 9.7).

CM PHASE

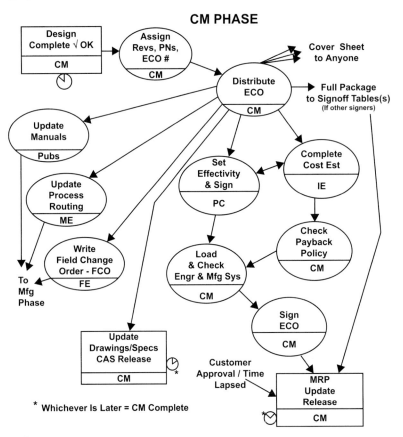

Figure 9.7 • CM phase flow diagram.

Some interesting features of this procedure flow should be noted. Most importantly, there is no CCB meeting here. The team meeting took place in the engineering phase where the team focused on the design documents and mark-ups of the design documents – exactly where technical reviews and signatures belong.

Also note that the process is not being held up for completion of the resulting manufacturing process changes, manual changes, field service orders, etc. The change *is* held for Production Control (PC) to make the effective date plan.

The completion of the cost estimate may not be practical until the effectivity of the change is planned. If the payback is not within policy, the change might be cancelled at this time – a rare occurrence by this procedure.

Notice that the CM organization is responsible for updating the master documents. This means that they must have control of the portion of the design/drafting people who are normally dedicated to updating masters. The reason this is strongly advised is that most designer/drafters would rather work on new development documents and routinely allow changes to age while doing so. Thus, the manpower is shifted to CM so that change can be a priority.

The manpower for updating the BOM and checking same is also in CM. This is for input of the design data and the effectivity plan data. Supply chain, production, accounting and other non-design data should be entered by those departments into the BOM system but not holding up the change. CM should verify timely entry as we discussed in the BOM process.

Some companies have the Operations folks enter the effective date and the BOM changes to the MRP/ERP system – probably because the Manufacturing folks purchased and installed that system. This is not best practice in this analyst's opinion because the BOM/parts lists are design documents. Thus the CM department should do the entry of design data to the system.

Note the "clocks" are placed so as to measure the time to update the BOM separately from the time to update the master documents. The CM phase will not be deemed complete until both are completed. As you will see, the metric for completion of the CM phase will be dependent upon "whichever is latest" but we can also measure each separately.

Manufacturing phase

This phase could also be labeled the "implementation phase." The efforts to complete this phase are fairly self-explanatory (see Fig. 9.8).

The clock for time measurement starts for this phase when the CM phase ended (later of updating the documents or the BOM) and does not end until the *actual* effective date or serial number is known – a shock to many. Thus we are positive that the implementation documentation changes and actual part changes are in the product. This also allows us to log the effective date/SN in appropriate file(s) for future troubleshooting or liability purposes.

Change process summary

Our entire procedure is now in flow diagram form – a picture being worth a thousand words. This will allow us to measure the thru-put time, volume and WIP at key points in the process. The process definition may

MANUFACTURING PHASE

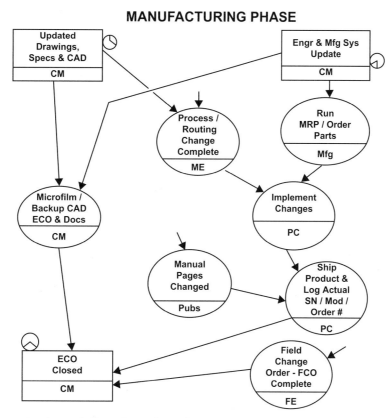

Figure 9.8 • Manufacturing or implementation phase flow diagram.

still require standards to define certain aspects of the workflow. Those standard numbers might well be placed on the flow diagram for quick reference.

Much of your workflow may be defined in a software system. Most of those systems have the ability to measure thru-put time, volume and WIP. Even if system defined, a workflow diagram(s) should still be part of your standards for training, management and improvement purposes.

- **Principle:** Flow diagramming the current process and measuring it are the first steps toward process improvement.

All phases of the change process involve team members from several departments. The processes have been named for the major contributor to that phase but the measurements cannot be thought of as measuring people or departments. The measurements will be of and about the process, its management and contributors as a whole. If the metrics are used as a whip on the back of people or departments the result will be very counter-productive.

Case study

Let's start this discussion with the most important metric in the change process – speed of the process. A Fortune 500 computer peripheral manufacturing company sensed a process time problem in their "money cow" division. They had few metrics except volume measurement – they were processing about 100 changes each month. They knew that the process was loaded with pain, suffering and complaints. Emotions ran high whenever the change process was discussed. Change Control Board meetings were fraught with arguments – even swearing. The new Executive VP of the division decided to take action. This analyst became involved.

They started by time measurement of a few major points in the process. They measured:

- Start
- Changed design input to Engineering Services
- Master docs updated
- BOM updated
- Effective date/SN known.

They found that the average process time was about:

- **38 work days** from start to giving the change to Engineering Services
- **40 work days** from change to Engineering Services to master docs and BOM updated
- **41 work days** from update to close (effective date or SN known).

This analyst referred to it as the "biblical 40–40–40" process – 40 work days and 40 nights for each major portion of the process. This was about two months for each phase or six months total. They decided to redesign the process with emphasis on reducing the middle 40 as it seemed most excessive.

A short meeting was held with all the people involved to explain the problem, discuss why speed was important and briefly explain the project. They put three key people to work with this analyst – one from Engineering Services, one from Materials and one from Operations.

Large 2 ft × 3 ft process time graphs were put on the wall in Engineering Services, in the cafeteria, outside the Chief Engineer's office and outside the Executive VP's office. A couple of weeks following the meeting, the process time decreased two or three days in every part of the process. The team had made no process changes as yet. Our conclusion was that when folks understand the importance of speed, they take it on themselves to help. Within another couple of weeks, a couple more days came off the front and rear portions of the process. The middle part of the process came down another six days – again, no changes to the process.

Another company saw similar but lesser results by adding to their EC form, in bold letters, "**Speed Without Sacrifice of Quality is Important to our Profitability and our Jobs.**"

- **Principle:** Measurement, in and of itself, tends to improve performance if given high visibility.

In the meantime the team was flow diagramming the current process and critiquing it. Many issues were identified, ranging from poor ECO form design to improper responsibility assignment. A sampling of changes and a data bank about those changes formed a further basis for improvement.

A team goal was set for improvement – reduce the middle portion of the process to five work days in the next year without increasing the front or rear thru-put time. The goal was then added to the graph. The die was cast. Cooperation was outstanding because the Chief Engineer and Executive VP co-chaired a steering committee, which received regular reports. They moved obstacles as they appeared in the team's path.

Details of this project can be found in the *EDC Handbook*. The metric for this project is shown in Fig. 9.9.

As you can see, the team essentially met its goal, albeit in more than a year. This performance was achieved with only two data processing systems – MRP and CAD. The CM process was what today would be referred to as a purely manual/hard copy system.

The front end and rear end of the process continued to increase in speed, not withstanding the fact that some tasks were removed from the middle and put up front or out back. Many companies achieve substantial

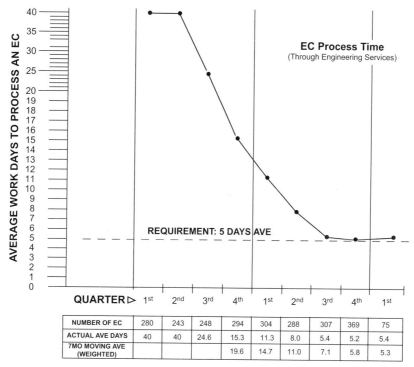

Figure 9.9 • Case study.

	1st	2nd	3rd	4th	1st	2nd	3rd	4th	1st
NUMBER OF EC	280	243	248	294	304	288	307	369	75
ACTUAL AVE DAYS	40	40	24.6	15.3	11.3	8.0	5.4	5.2	5.4
7MO MOVING AVE (WEIGHTED)				19.6	14.7	11.0	7.1	5.8	5.3

improvement in their process time, but none this writer is aware of without first defining the process flow and measuring it.

Want a fast change process with high-quality documentation and high-quality changes? Define the workflow – then series of metrics are in order. Each part of the process should be measured with regard to thru-put time and volume. This measurement might be done monthly if you are satisfied with the performance. That monthly report would be labeled Silver or Bronze. If the thru-put time performance is not improving or is deemed too long, then the metrics should be called Gold and done weekly.

Engineering phase metrics

As noted before, the change process should begin with the acceptance of the request – no void between the request and the change processes. If some requests bypass the request process they should still "go thru" CM. In that fashion CM can know when the change was actually started. Changes initiated in Engineering would require the start date to be identified by management. The engineering phase of the process should look something like Fig. 9.5. Measurement of the process time should be the first metric as in Fig. 9.10.

The process time performance is coming down while the volume of changes is rising. This appears to be a good trend – and it is. However, could this positive trend be occurring while the quantity of changes in WIP is growing? If that were to occur, there would certainly be trouble ahead (see Fig. 9.11).

These are the same process time and volume data as in Fig. 9.10 with the work in process added. In this unusual condition the WIP is growing, not withstanding the improved process time and slight increases in the volume completed. One device manufacturer had this very condition. Analysis showed that there was no

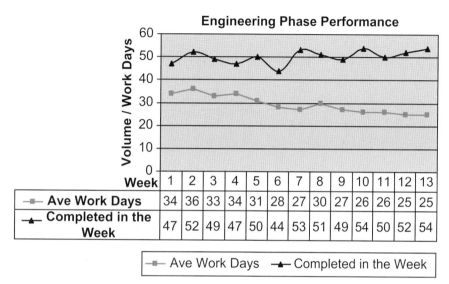

Engineering Phase Performance

Week	1	2	3	4	5	6	7	8	9	10	11	12	13
Ave Work Days	34	36	33	34	31	28	27	30	27	26	26	25	25
Completed in the Week	47	52	49	47	50	44	53	51	49	54	50	52	54

Figure 9.10 • Engineering process metrics.

request process and the decision as to which changes to work on was left to the design engineers. They assigned a start date when they decided to address the issue – not an unreasonable position. That date was not, however, when the change first arrived in engineering. Thus, a void existed between the request and change processes. They were working on those issues that seemed important to them or were relatively easy to fix, or that they were directed to address. The WIP was growing, requestors were unhappy and the

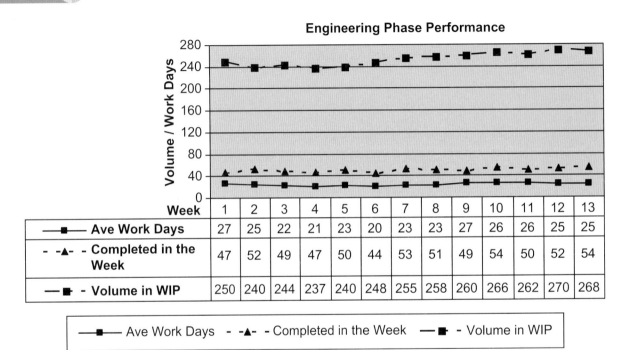

Engineering Phase Performance

Week	1	2	3	4	5	6	7	8	9	10	11	12	13
——■—— Ave Work Days	27	25	22	21	23	20	23	23	27	26	26	25	25
- -▲- - Completed in the Week	47	52	49	47	50	44	53	51	49	54	50	52	54
——■- Volume in WIP	250	240	244	237	240	248	255	258	260	266	262	270	268

——■—— Ave Work Days - -▲- - Completed in the Week ——■- Volume in WIP

Figure 9.11 ● Engineering process metrics with WIP.

problems festered. Many of the "changes" backlogged in WIP were actually requests in limbo. The requestor thought that Engineering had taken ownership but Engineering merely thought of them as being in a "queue" to be addressed later, or not. No mechanism was in place to reject requests.

The engineers felt that the process time should start when they took ownership of the problem. The amount of time the "requests" were in limbo wasn't measured. This example highlights the need for a request process, and the need to measure WIP and to start the change measurement when the request is approved.

The average time through the engineering phase in this case (given the start dates recognized by the engineers) is about 25 work days – five weeks. Is this time excessive, typical or fast? This analyst has seen times that vary from one to 14 weeks. There is no "typical" as such. Every company should ask what the typical or normal might be for their environment. It depends upon the complexity of the product, the technology, the testing required, etc. The best approach is probably to measure the time and expect constant improvement under the principle that every man-made process can be improved by man.

Goals for improvement might be set in increments – perhaps two or three days at a time. If that is done, the goal should be clearly labeled "interim" or some such terminology.

Point of no return metrics

This process begins when the engineer sends or brings/sends the change into CM as in Fig. 9.6. It ends when the check list has been successfully passed. As mentioned before, the check should take place within one hour. The metric for this event should be similar to Fig. 9.12.

Of course the check point is just the first step in the CM phase of the change process. It is important to measure it separately because it must happen very fast if the engineers are to learn that speed is important. Also it is measured separately because the time will be charged to the engineering phase if the check list is not passed.

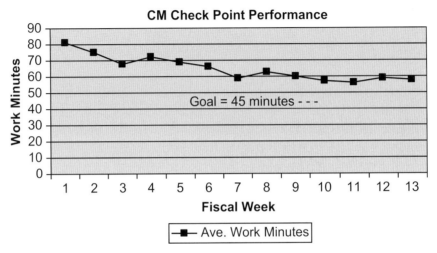

Figure 9.12 • Check point performance measurement.

In this example the goal was not met. There has been improvement up to the tenth week but little progress since. This condition needs to be analyzed. Such analysis should start quickly lest the people involved begin to feel that speed is not that important. If no immediate improvements in the process can be found the goal should be re-examined. Of course, improvement is always possible but priorities may not allow time for improving this process. If the policy says it must happen within one hour average, the prudent action may be to reset the goal to one hour.

If and when any change is accepted by CM, that change (and the time to check/accept it) automatically enters the CM phase.

CM phase metrics

The CM phase flow diagram in Fig. 9.7 might be named the "administrative/technical phase." The design work has been completed, reviewed and approved. All involved need to be informed about the progress of each change. The technical tasks of planning the change effective date/SN, incorporating the change in the master documents and incorporating the change into the BOM need to be accomplished.

These tasks need to be performed quickly and accurately. The speed should be measured starting from the engineering phase complete to update of both the master documents and the BOM. One company measured and graphed the speed and listed their change volume on the metric. They did this monthly. The result is shown in Fig. 9.13.

This company found that measuring and publishing this time graph for the CM phase along with documenting the process and training those involved had resulted in some improvement – not withstanding a slight growth in the volume of changes. They were not satisfied with the 20-work-day situation and the slight improvement, however. They determined to:

- Increase the frequency of reporting to weekly and
- Set a goal for thru-put time of ten work days.

That weekly measurement looked something like Fig. 9.14.

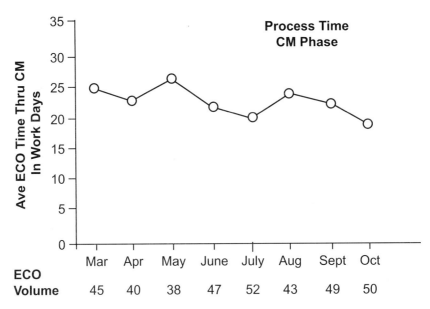

Figure 9.13 • Change time – case study.

The measurement was done weekly – the process time thru CM did continue to improve, albeit slightly. This electronic product company decided to examine the update time for both documents and the BOM – separately. They suspected that one or both were excessive.

The lapsed time to set effective dates was included with the time to update the BOM. The resultant metrics looked like Figs 9.15 and 9.16.

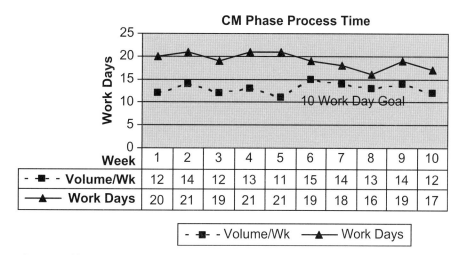

CM Phase Process Time

Week	1	2	3	4	5	6	7	8	9	10
- ■ - **Volume/Wk**	12	14	12	13	11	15	14	13	14	12
▲ **Work Days**	20	21	19	21	21	19	18	16	19	17

- ■ - Volume/Wk   ▲ Work Days

Figure 9.14 • Case study – weekly metric with goal set.

The condition experienced by this company is not unusual. The drafting/designer folks would rather work on new designs than work on change incorporation. In this case the Engineering Services Director divided the design drafters into two groups – new design and change incorporation based on an analysis of their logged time data. The portion doing change incorporation were put to work directly for the CM manager. They did not physically move. The less experienced design drafters were put in CM because incorporation of changes was considered better training ground. The Engineering Services Director shifted people on a temporary basis, if/as necessary to match the workload of new vs. change.

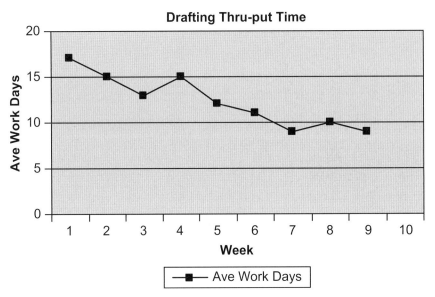

Figure 9.15 ● Time for drafting change incorporation.

The initial reduction from 25 to 20 work days took seven months. After measuring and reporting weekly, a meager three days were removed from the process. After measuring and reporting on the document update and BOM update separately and establishing competition between the groups involved, it only took another seven weeks to meet their ten-work-day goal. No new people were added to the process. The quality of changes improved as measured by a method we will discuss later.

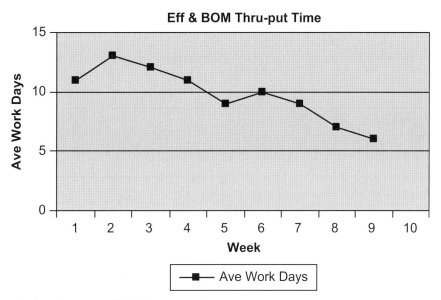

Figure 9.16 • Time for effective date and BOM incorporation.

The Director of Engineering Services instituted a new hiring policy. New people were hired into CM (Update Drafting) and someone was normally promoted to the New Design Drafting Group. The feedback to this analyst indicated that everyone was happy with the outcome.

The importance of these metrics deserves the initial Gold designation. When the goals have been met, the department should have a party, toot their horn and lower the importance ranking to Silver. Another goal of five or six work days might be set. The separate measurement of the drafting and BOM incorporation might well be discontinued when the goal is met.

The changes now progress into the incorporation or manufacturing process.

Manufacturing phase metrics

The manufacturing phase begins with the update of the design documents and the BOM (whichever is later), as noted in Fig. 9.8. The fact is, however, that much of their work can begin when the CM functions notifies manufacturing of the change passing the check point (Fig. 9.7). They can proceed with mark-ups to estimate costs, schedule work, revise processes, revise manuals and to start the field change process. The Supply Chain folks can obtain supplier estimates, pick a supplier and even write or revise purchase orders.

The end of this phase is the notification of CM by manufacturing (probably PC) of the actual effective date/SN. One required measurement of this phase would be total thru-put time, as in Fig. 9.17.

This metric is labeled Gold because the time and volume are increasing. Some corrective action is needed. Possibly a request process needs to be put in place. Perhaps a goal should be set and communicated to all in the manufacturing phase. What is a reasonable goal for this phase? This writer has no benchmark for manufacturing process time. A good deal depends upon the existing inventory, disposition of old design parts and urgency of the change.

The time it should take to order parts, receive, inspect, stock, issue, build, test, etc. is dependent upon the complexity of the product, the manufacturing process, the stock status, the disposition on the old

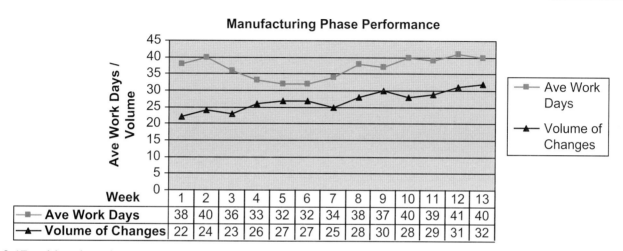

Manufacturing Phase Performance

Week	1	2	3	4	5	6	7	8	9	10	11	12	13
Ave Work Days	38	40	36	33	32	32	34	38	37	40	39	41	40
Volume of Changes	22	24	23	26	27	27	25	28	30	28	29	31	32

Figure 9.17 • Manufacturing phase time and volume metric.

design parts, whether make or buy parts are affected, etc. One would surmise that it would normally take longer to do those things than to update the process, tooling, and manuals and to complete a field change order if required. In any event it is probably the Operations VP's call as to what is a reasonable average time and to set goals.

Certainly the increasing process time indicated in this graph is of concern and should be "bubbled up" thru the operations chain of command. This condition may be caused by a number of different issues. The Operations VP must be made aware of the situation and the trend.

It may be appropriate to measure certain elements of this phase – publications/manuals, field change, process/tooling, etc. That responsibility should be with the CM manager since those elements may affect the total change process time.

Total change process time

The total process time should be summarized, probably by display of the three phases' average times. Of all the metrics shown in this chapter, this summary metric CM would be the place to start. This metric might initially be produced monthly in bar chart form, as shown in Fig. 9.18.

This metric should be continued as Gold regardless of the performance. It should be done weekly if the total time or any of the phases seem excessive. Other metrics covered above should follow if the total time or phase times seem excessive – obviously starting with the phase that seems most out of line.

- **Principle:** "As a strategic weapon, time is the equivalent of money, productivity, quality, even innovation."

  (*Harvard Business Review*: "Time – The Next Source of Competitive Advantage")

We must, of course, be careful not to speed up the process by "hurrying up to do it wrong." For this reason it is very important that we find a way to measure the quality of the process.

Change process quality

There are many people and functions involved in all phases of the change process. If people are prone to make 2–3% error (as learned somewhere in the writer's ME/IE training) then several people involved in one

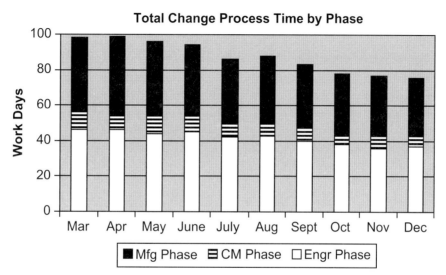

Figure 9.18 • Total change process time by phase.

phase can produce a double-digit error level fairly quickly. Also, many companies have processes that produce a culture that says:

- **Negative principle:** We can't find time to do it right, but we can always find time to do it over.

Many companies have two or more methods of making a "fast change" to be followed later by the "formal process." Often the formal change that follows is a different configuration than the fast change. Generally the fast method isn't tracked to date/SN. Sometimes the formal change never happens. These are all conditions that invite lawyers to feast on the company treasures should any remotely related product failure result in injury or worse.

The best method to prevent errors is to have well-trained people. Standards must be available for a basis of training. The next step is to require each person in the process trained to check the work of the person preceding them in the process. The best solution to prevention of the multiple methods for making fast changes is to make the normal change process fast – then to eliminate the other "fast change" methods.

The best practice for measuring process quality that this analyst has witnessed is measurement of error corrections. This would include revisions to a change in process and a change to correct an earlier change.

Corrections should be divided into two parts:

1. Design error corrections:
   - Fixes to the design fix after the mark-ups have been signed
   - ECOs to correct design errors in earlier ECOs.

2. Administrative and technical error corrections:
   - Fixes to the administrative aspects of change document after distribution of the change
   - *Excludes* changes/re-plan to the effectivity dates
   - Document only corrections after incorporation of the change into the design documents or BOM

- Error found in the incorporation of the changes to the design documents or BOM, whether corrected by revising the change in process or by another ECO (mark-ups not changed – error made in incorporation of mark-ups).

Needless to say, any revisions to the change document should be flagged in some obvious manner, revision dated and the change redistributed.

  With those definitions in mind, the CM folks should merely count the number of each error found in a week or month and compare that to the number of changes made during the same timeframe – the result being a quality control, or QC, factor. For example:

Design Process Quality: 5 fixes this month ÷ 20 changes this month
$\times 100 = 25\%$ Design QC Factor

Admin/Tech Process Quality: 4 admin revs this month ÷ 20 changes this month
$\times 100 = 20\%$ Tech QC Factor

It must be recognized that there is potential evil in these metrics. It is all too simplistic to interpret them as a measure of design engineers, design departments, the CM department or the design group as a whole. This is bad reasoning. There are far too many people and departments involved in the process to say that it measures one person or one department. For example, the manufacturing engineer might belatedly decide that the tolerance on a dimension should be tighter or looser. The design engineer agrees but must change a mark-up already signed. Should that revision be called the design engineer's responsibility? Perhaps the ME didn't communicate with the proper team member. Perhaps the ME wasn't on the team and should be. Perhaps the ME didn't do the review ahead of the meeting but, rather, after the meeting. Perhaps the design engineer pressured the ME to sign and later decided the request was actually valid. Perhaps, perhaps, perhaps ... ad nauseam. Thus:

- **Principle:** The QC factor quality measurement must be about measuring the process, not the people or functions.

The quality control factor must be presented and thought of as a measure of the change process – each factor relating to its applicable phase (see Figs 9.19 and 9.20).

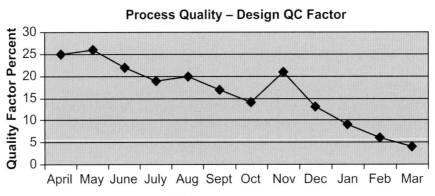

Process Quality – Design QC Factor

Figure 9.19 • Process quality measurement, design QC factor.

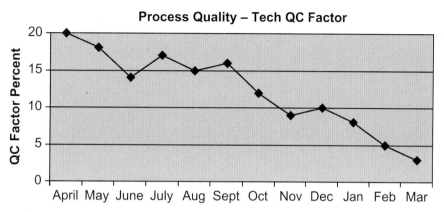

Figure 9.20 • Process quality measurement – tech QC factor.

Companies that have measured the process quality in this fashion have been surprised to find the factor in the 15–25% range. This means that they are doing about a fifth of their changes over again because the engineering design phase of the process has some deficiency(ies).

In this writer's experience, errors in this process are attributable to "all of the above." In other words, many different process issues exist. One of the major contributors, however, is having folks sign the change document instead of the mark-up. When eyes focus on marked-up documents, results improve.

Again, the companies that have used this metric report that they find about a fifth of their changes are re-done in the CM phase or after for administrative/technical corrections. This means that this phase of the process needs improvement. One of the major contributors is *lack of a technical release/ point of no return* (see the *EDC Handbook* for many other contributors to change process errors).

The process improvements to reduce the error levels are not easy – or accomplished in a short time. The scale of one year shown in these graphs may be optimistic depending upon management involvement.

The manufacturing phase of the process is generally well covered with quality assurance measurements. The single addition to their arsenal, if not there already, would be tracking of "bad parts" to the root cause. It would be very interesting to find out what portion of the rejected, scrapped, reworked and returned-to-supplier parts have "documentation issues" as the root cause. That is, when are CM issues the root cause of "bad parts?"

This analyst has heard people blame management, management blame people, people blame other people and management blame other management for errors made. The problems usually lie in the processes, however. Remember our first principle:

- **Principle:** Processes are the very essence of business.

The answers, my friend, are *not* blowing in the wind – they are *embedded* in the processes. The few companies that have measured and improved their change process quality have achieved single-digit QC factors – some to 2–3% – and often with process time reductions.

Benchmarking survey – change process

For comparison the applicable portion of the benchmarking survey is as follows:

Changes made per week: 22 average.

Ways to make a design change are (check all applicable):

Quick change form followed by formal change form 29%

Deviation/waiver form followed by formal change form 50%

Mark-ups on production floor 23%

Change form is only way to make design changes 76%

Other 10% – hold order, QC form, MRB response, PCR, revised drawings.

Total number of ways to make a change: 2.4 average, range 1–4.

Normal use of change form: See Fig. 9.21.

Comment: If you don't normally use the one problem/one fix/one change form method how do you know if your volume is increasing or decreasing, how do you benchmark with others, how do you compare groups or products? If several problems can normally be fixed with one form, where does it end and how slow is your process?

It is clear as to whom EDC/CM can accept a change from:

Yes – any engineer 71%

Yes – specific engineers 11%

No 18%.

Problem / Fix / Form Relationship

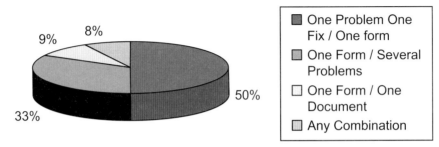

Figure 9.21 • Normal use of change form.

Comment: If you accept a change from "any engineer," do you really have meaning for the term "cognizant/responsible/engineer"? Who is responsible for the design? Isn't "any engineer" a committee design?

It is clear as to when the request process ends and the change process begins:
Yes 75%
No 25%.

Comment: To test this in your company, try asking someone from Engineering, Manufacturing and QA to identify that point and see if they all agree!

We have a CCB (Change Control Board):
Yes 49%
No 51%.

Number of people who regularly attend the CCB: 7.2 average, range 4–15, CCBs per week 1.6.

Length of the typical CCB: 1.2 hours.

Is typical CCB held:
  As soon as the problem is recognized
  After the engineer is complete
  Other _____
  NA.
Comment: Question poorly asked. Should have said: "When in the change process is the change first presented to the board?" Answers thus are meaningless.

Opinion – CCB functions well:
  Yes 64%
  No 36%.
Comment: After discussion about CCBs, seminar attendees generally agree that they are held too late in the process.

Number of changes typically in process: 32.6 average, range 3–300.
Comment: 22 average completed per week (first question in change process) would queue-calculate to 1.5 weeks of thru-put time – 32.6 in process ÷ 22 per week = 1.5 weeks. The question was poorly asked because we don't know which part of the process people answered this question for. I suspect that most were referring to "doc control" excluding those in "re-design" or "update masters" queue.

Number of signatures on the typical change form: 5.4 average, range 1–12.

Change form is called:
ECO 16
ECN 14
Three companies or fewer – DAN, ADCN, PCO, ECP, EDCR, ECR, EO, EC, EA, CO, EDCF, ECF, EDC, EAR, DLO, REA.

Change form is:
Online 13%
Hard copy 65%
Both 22%.

Signatures are online:
Yes 13%
No 87%.
Comment: Today we would find a much higher proportion of companies online.

Change form hard copies distributed per month: _____

Average pages in a change package: _____
Comment: Answers indicate that these two questions were not understood. Best method – distribute the ECO form (preferably online) and require those who need prints to pull their prints when needed.

Are all pages in the package distributed when the change form is distributed:
Yes 59%
No 27%
Sometimes 14%.

In the change package, it is easy to tell if the change is:
Interchangeable
Non-interchangeable
Doc only
All three 59%
Document only 33%
None 8%.
Comment: The subjective word is "easy."

EDC/CM group has in-department resources to revise master docs as a result of changes: See Fig. 9.22.
Comment: Question didn't ask if resources are used – always, sometimes, etc. Answers may therefore be skewed. When CM has the ability and responsibility to incorporate changes into the masters, the process is always faster. Doing updates by CM requires the change to be fully documented by mark-up and/or "was–is" detail. The question also didn't ask where in the process this is done – before the point of no return or after.

If Yes on prior question, which docs were/had:
Pictorials hand drawn 46%
Pictorials CAD drawn 57%

CM Resources to Master Up-Date

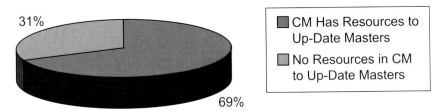

31%

69%

CM Has Resources to Up-Date Masters

No Resources in CM to Up-Date Masters

Figure 9.22 • EDC/CM group has in-department resources to revise master docs as a result of changes.

Word processed 51%
Other 2%.
Comment: See BOM section for BOM/PL input by Doc Control/CM.

The change is specifically defined in the change package by:
Marked prints 84%
Was–is/now description 62%
New condition (refer to old print for "was" condition) 19%
Not specifically defined – compare old and new docs 10%
Other (undefined) 3%.

Flag "notes" are used on the revised docs:
Yes 49%
No 51%.

Change package is sent to the supplier affected:
Yes 70%
No 30%.
Comment: Why keep the detailed description of the change from your supplier? It only causes them to compare the old and new prints (usually on a light table) and to make mistakes in doing so.

Effectivity of our changes is set/managed by:
CCB 24%
Production Control/Materials 50%
ME 22%
Other 12% – 3 Engineering, 2 Purchasing, 1 Marketing, 1 PC and ME.
Comment: Some checked more than one box.

Disposition of old design parts is done on the change form:
Yes 73%
No 7%
Sometimes 20%.

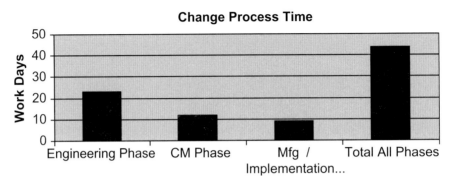

Figure 9.23 ● Change process time by phase.

We precisely measure the change process time:

Yes 31%

No 69%.

Comment: Only four were willing to furnish their report.

Change process time by phase: See Fig. 9.23.

Comment: Most CM organizations consider implementation to be complete upon documents being revised and/or distributed. The answers for "implementation" would indicate this belief. If implementation time were precisely measured, it would probably be considerably larger. Since less than a third of the companies claimed to "precisely" measure the process time, these data must be treated as largely estimated as opposed to measured. The author's experience would say that all average process time numbers are optimistic/guesses/estimates.

Chapter Ten

Field change metrics

Some companies incorporate engineering changes into units already shipped. The rules under which this is done are often unwritten and therefore vague and variable by whim. Often the Field Service organization unilaterally decides which changes to put into units shipped, on what basis and when. Sometimes policies exist that are themselves counter-productive.

One mainframe computer company had a policy to retrofit "every shipped unit to the latest change." This policy made sense early in the product's lifecycle because almost every early change was made to meet specifications. Later in the product lifecycle few changes were to meet specs and many were to improve the product or reduce costs. Is a cost reduction retrofitted a real cost reduction? No – it is actually a cost adder! Should units already shipped be retrofitted to add improvements? Probably not. Analysis revealed that the policy was unwritten – folklore. This company reconsidered and documented its policy regarding field changes and saved over a million dollars a year – in 1967 dollars.

Another company had the policy of upgrading any unit returned to the factory for repair, to the latest configuration. It was a "like new" policy – also highly questionable. Examination showed that such a repaired unit was 10–20% more costly than a new unit if a fair value was given to the returned unit.

This analyst would not consider any interchangeable change for field retrofit. Not all non-interchangeable changes would be retrofit by field change order (FCO). Repair in the field or factory would be limited to worn, damaged or failed parts and FCOs – sometimes with quotation for cost/price recovery as appropriate.

The decision as to which non-interchangeable changes would merit an FCO would be made by the change team and indicated on the engineering change document (ECO). The Field Service organization must be part of that team. This is necessary in order to have the proper people make the FCO decision and to have the costs included in the payback analysis when appropriate.

Field change standards

As usual, the first step is to identify the policy and procedure for retrofit, repair, returns and refurbishment, a subject this writer will oversimplify as "field change" – changes after initial shipment. The needed standards in this arena are:

Field Change Policy – Which changes will be installed during retrofit, repair, etc.   Yes ☐   No ☐

Field Change Form – Disassembly, reassembly, test, disposition of old parts, etc.   Yes ☐   No ☐

Form Instructions – Box-by-box form instruction or cursor pop-up instruction.   Yes ☐   No ☐

Process Flow Diagram – Procedural sequence of events and responsibilities.   Yes ☐   No ☐

Field change process flow

The FCO process flow responsible departments are indicated in the abbreviated flow along with a brief description of the major events. The presumption in this diagram is that there is a Publications organization with technical writer(s) who will write the FCO. It will contain the disassembly, reassembly, test and disposition of old design parts. Part of the FCO will be a kit of parts. Other standards might be required in order to define individual events (see Fig. 10.1).

Note that one FCO installation is done/checked by a person other than the writer. They use a copy of the FCO and a kit of parts. This avoids the "Christmas Eve syndrome" wherein the instruction is not easily understood and the kit contains fewer or more parts than are required.

It is critical that the knowledge of installation serial number by serial number be fed back to the factory – either to CM or where CM and engineers have ready access to the field configuration. This can be done online or simply by putting a self-addressed postcard in the kit. This is critical information for the engineer's future troubleshooting.

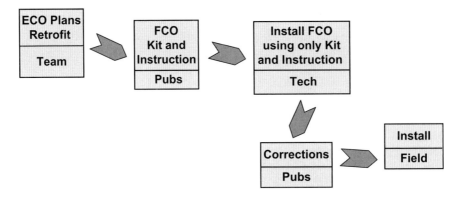

Figure 10.1 • Field change order process flow.

Field change order metrics

Any company that has a serious safety issue will institute a "recall" FCO and normally make it happen fast. This is a unique situation wherein the units will be "recalled" for retrofit and taken out of service because of the critical nature of the FCO – a safety issue. They will take very unique steps to avoid liability issues, such as advertising or requesting a public service announcement on radio or TV. The rest of the FCOs are often done leisurely. This may be fine if the customer's best interest is dictating that priority. However, the creation and processing of the FCO and making it available to the field/customer is something that should happen fast, regardless of the field priority. This gives the customer/field service the alternative to install the change quickly or not as they wish.

After the ECO is specified to result in an FCO (and the check point of no return is passed) the tech writer can begin FCO preparation – the start process. After the FCO is communicated to the field, the time measurement can end (see Fig. 10.2).

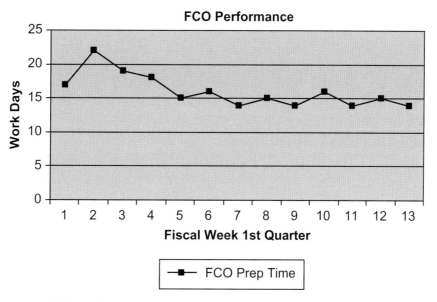

Figure 10.2 • Time to prepare FCO and issue to the field.

In this case the Loader Company prepared and published the metric, and it apparently had an immediate effect to slightly improve the timeliness of the FCO. Recognizing that 15 work days (three weeks) probably isn't reasonable for these events, a process improvement project needs to be undertaken – and a goal should be set. Companies have written the FCO, entered a kit in the BOM, test installed, corrected the FCO and distributed it to the field in about a week. A goal of five to seven work days would be reasonable.

The elements of this process might be measured separately, but this should only be a temporary measure to identify where the most time is used. Again, many people are involved in the process and the best approach is therefore to measure the process as a whole – not the people. A field change quality factor could be developed, measured and graphed in a metric – corrections to FCO or kits compared to the number of FCOs in the same timeframe.

Field installation performance

The time to issue the FCO, install it and feed that information back to the factory should also be measured – probably by the Service organization. In some companies field service is organized in Engineering, thus probably putting CM in the installation measurement business. Since the installation data are primarily for engineering troubleshooting purposes, CM must make sure that this knowledge is available to the engineer – as promptly as is practical.

For any given FCO this arena gets somewhat more complicated because some units may not be changed for some time and more units may be put in the field before the change is made in production. Thus it is important to measure both the time and the percentage of units with or without each specific FCO (see Fig. 10.3).

Since this metric is needed on every FCO, it can become quite a burden. A data processing report may be a better solution if a company has very many FCOs.

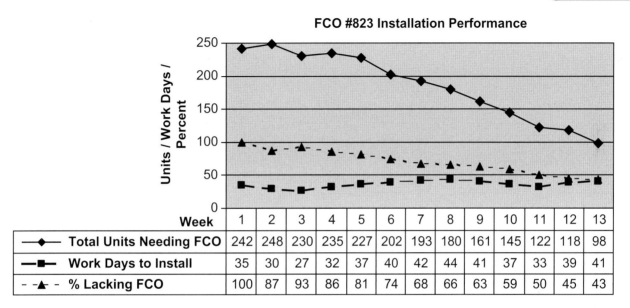

FCO #823 Installation Performance

Week	1	2	3	4	5	6	7	8	9	10	11	12	13
◆ Total Units Needing FCO	242	248	230	235	227	202	193	180	161	145	122	118	98
■ Work Days to Install	35	30	27	32	37	40	42	44	41	37	33	39	41
▲ % Lacking FCO	100	87	93	86	81	74	68	66	63	59	50	45	43

Figure 10.3 • FCO # 823 installation performance.

Between the Service organization and CM there should be a database that will show the engineer what serial numbers (SNs) have the change and which don't – again for troubleshooting purposes. This might be made part of the "as-built" configuration database or a separate database. In both cases it is necessary for the engineer to be able to easily find out what SN has the change installed. In this case the field data have been added to the manufacturing effective SN database. This database contains only the non-interchangeable changes – which we will trace to SN (limited data are shown as space allows; see Table 10.1). This is a perpetually Gold report – called "status accounting" by DOD folks.

Table 10.1 SN affected by non-interchangeable changes

ECO number	Title of change	Manufacturing SN effective	FCO number	Field SNs w/FCO	As of date
1384	First-aid kit moved	128 and up	NA		2 Sept
1385	Operator ladder added	133 and up	823	101, 102, 104, 105, …	4 Sept
1286	Blade material titanium	135, 137, 139 and up	824	102, 103, 104, 106, …	2 Sept
1287	Improve wipers	123 and up	NA		4 Sept
1291	Wider tires and wheel	136 and up	NA		12 Sept
1292	New engine idle chip	123, 125 and up	825	125, 126, 127, …	4 Sept
1293	Reduce bucket cost	141 and up	NA		12 Sept

When failures occur, the SNs of failed units must be identified. The engineer can then search the potentially affected part or assembly documents to identify ECO numbers (and deviations) that may be involved. The engineer can go to this database and see whether or not the changes involved may have caused the problem – or fixed it.

Notice that only non-interchangeable changes are tracked (commercial practices) in the database. If the engineer thinks that an *interchangeable* change may have something to do with a failure, they can look at the ECO to find out the approximate date the change was effective.

Notice also that not all non-interchangeable changes are retrofit. Careful decisions as to which are and aren't to be retrofit should be done in the ECO process.

Field change volume

From time to time – perhaps twice a year – the CM manager should take a snapshot of changes to see how many of the non-interchangeable changes are approved for retrofit. They might be changes that are required to meet specs, offered for sale as a feature or only to be installed "upon failure" or "upon repair," etc. The Loader Company has the following categories for non-interchangeable changes:

- No FCO required
- FCO recall
- FCO only upon failure
- FCO at regular maintenance
- FCO installed upon repair, retrofit or refurbishment/for sale.

We need to measure the breakdown of non-interchangeable ECOs by category of FCO. A snapshot for the first half of last year might look like Fig. 10.4.

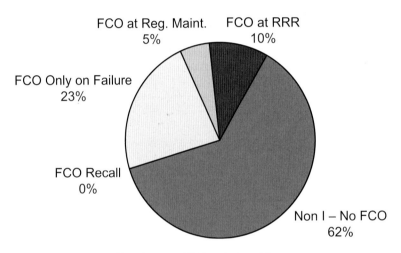

Non-Interchangeable Change Disposition

FCO at Reg. Maint. 5%

FCO at RRR 10%

FCO Only on Failure 23%

FCO Recall 0%

Non I – No FCO 62%

Figure 10.4 • First half-year non-interchangeable change–FCO relationship.

These data, although interesting, are relatively meaningless. They certainly show that the team has been fairly diligent about limiting the changes that are to become FCOs. To look again at the breakdown in the second half of the year might be interesting (see Fig. 10.5).

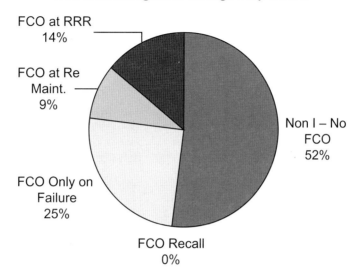

Non-Interchangeable Change Disposition

FCO at RRR
14%

FCO at Re
Maint.
9%

Non I – No
FCO
52%

FCO Only on
Failure
25%

FCO Recall
0%

Figure 10.5 • Second half-year non-interchangeable change–FCO relationship.

Standing alone these data are still fairly meaningless. However, if we compare the first half to the second half of the year we can see a "shift" that should raise some concern. The percentage of non-interchangeable changes not to be field changed has decreased from 62 to 52. This means 10% more FCOs – certainly a trend that should be analyzed.

It should also cause CM to increase the frequency of reporting and to change from a pie chart to a bar chart or line graph. As stated before, this writer prefers the timeline graph (see Fig. 10.6).

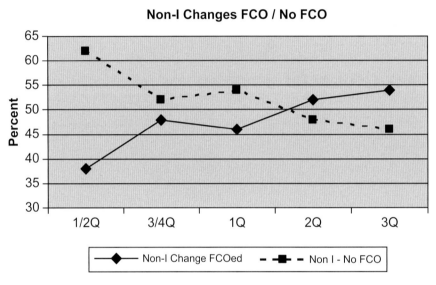

Figure 10.6 ● FCO trend.

It shouldn't take too many quarters with this trend before CM would upgrade the importance to Gold. Presentation of the data in this simplistic manner should get management's attention. This trend is certainly alarming. Costs will increase significantly.

One mechanical–hydraulic device manufacturer found this trend, investigated and found a "team dynamics" issue. The field service engineer was a powerful personality and saw his role on the team to have more changes retrofit. Their management injected the Chief Engineer into the change process to make the final decision as to whether or not an FCO was required. The trend immediately reversed – at considerable savings. Guidelines were eventually established that allowed the Chief Engineer to withdraw from the process.

Benchmarking survey – field changes

For comparison the applicable portion of the benchmarking survey is as follows:

Some changes are field installed:
  Yes 67%
  No 33%.

Some changes are installed on product return:
  Yes 79%
  No 21%.

EDC/CM has record of the effectivity of changes:
  Factory installed – Yes 50%, No 50%
  Field installed – Yes 29%, No 71%
  Repair installed – Yes 32%, No 68%.

Comment: The preferred condition would be that Doc Control has the effectivity of all changes. If Doc Control doesn't know the effectivity, they should certainly know where to get it.

Chapter Eleven

11

Definitions

Sometimes the dictionary is lacking. Every discipline has its unique terminology. In the CM world, "effectivity" is a classic example. Instead of saying that we need to trace the change to the date it was effective, we simply say we need to track the effectivity. Although this author tries to avoid use of acronyms or unique terms, it seems almost unavoidable. Then with the exploding use of information technology (IT) automating processes, the need for definition multiplies. Critical to any process documentation are three kinds of definition:

- Data dictionary definitions
- Acronyms explained (especially for new employees)
- Terms defined.

Each can be treated separately or combined in groups. How that is done is arbitrary. For this work the data dictionary will be one entity and the acronyms and terms another. This is simply because the author has no data dictionary to offer – only the concept.

Data dictionary

In this age of multiple software programs, it is important for every company to develop a digital definition of every frequently referenced data element. The larger a company gets, the more important this becomes. A seminar attendee from a government research organization relayed a confirmation of this need. He indicated that they have found over 20 different digital definitions of a part number – a touch of insanity. Every company should develop one digital definition for a part number as early in its life as possible.

Example: **Part number**

eight digits	all numeric
first six digits	sequentially assigned
last two digits	version of the part number – tab or dash

The need for definition of dates has long been recognized. Other data such as item number, quantity, revision level all need a digital definition in the data dictionary in order to avoid duplicate definitions. This data dictionary should be jointly developed by CM, Information Technology, and the Policy and Procedure function. It might be combined with, or separate from, the acronyms and definitions for CM standards development.

Acronyms and terms

Most disciplines have a set of frequently used acronyms, unique words and terms. Acronyms, words and terms used in the seminars taught by the author are included in this listing. Sources are usually identified if not common or his own. Terms used are not defined when the definition is fairly universally understood (Webster). Other definitions appear in the APICS Dictionary, in MIL standards and in ISO standards.

Assembly   Any item with a parts list.

Benchmark   A fixed point of reference or a standard for comparison. An outstanding example that is appropriate for use as a model.

Block diagram   An illustration in which essential elements of any system are drawn in the form of blocks and their relationship(s) to each other are indicated by appropriate interconnecting lines and arrows.

BOD   Bill Of Documents. A compilation of the specifications, procedures, and other records that are needed in the design, manufacture or maintenance of a product but do not represent a part. Might include the drawing numbers for product parts if the drawings are identified with a number not identical to or embedded in the part number.

BOM   Bill Of Material. A compilation of the parts lists for an assembly or a product – may be displayed in a variety of formats. DOD terms:

As-designed BOM – a DOD term that means different things to different people

As-planned BOM – a DOD term that means different things to different people

As-built BOM – a DOD term that means different things to different people

As-shipped BOM – a DOD term that means different things to different people

As-maintained BOM – a DOD term that means different things to different people.

See DOD specs for stated meanings. Realize that one might be talking about a BOM for each unit of product or a BOM for each order of product, etc. Also keep in mind that MRP/ERP systems generally reflect effectivity dates (planned or actual) the time wherein the old design part will no longer be issued from stock and the new designed part will. Such a date may have little resemblance to the date of build or shipment.

CAD   Computer-Aided Design/Drafting. Computer tools used to assist in the creation and maintenance of configuration-design definition and documentation. Source: *EIT Glossary*.

CAE   Computer-Aided Engineering. Computer tools used to design and conduct analytical tests on design models. Source: *EIT Glossary*.

CAM   Computer-Aided Manufacturing. Computer tools (which may be capable of extracting and utilizing the CAD data) used to assist in the creation and maintenance of the methods used to produce the item. Source: *EIT Glossary*.

CCB   Change Control Board or Configuration Control Board. A team of people too often involved too late in the change process.

CDR   Critical Design Review.

CDRL Contract Data Requirements List.

CIM Computer Integrated Manufacturing.

Class I Categorization of non-interchangeable changes *and other changes* as defined by the DOD.

Class II Categorization of product changes that are not class I.

CM Configuration Management. A simple, fast, accurate, systematic, efficient and well-understood process approach/discipline for planning, identifying, controlling and tracking a product's configuration throughout its life. *Source:* Frank Watts.

Configuration Management (CM) A field of management that focuses on establishing and maintaining consistency of a product's performance and its functional and physical attributes with its requirements, design and operational information throughout its life. Source: *Wikipedia*.

CNC Computer Numerical Control.

Concurrent engineering A management/operational approach meant to improve product design, production, operation and maintenance by developing environments in which personnel from all disciplines (Design, Marketing, Production Engineering, Process Planning, and Support) work together and share data throughout all phases of the product lifecycle. Source: *EIT Glossary*.

Configurator Software tools that simplify order entry by asking which features and options the customer wants; then they may apply predefined rules to correctly configure the product with the desired attributes, and/or test for rules conflict, and/or launch the order, and may generate the BOM, routing and price. Source: R. Bourke, Bourke Associates.

Database　A collection of structured data elements that are application independent.

Data element　The smallest pieces of data that cannot be subdivided and still retain any meaning. The terms "data item" and "data field" or simply "field" are often used synonymously with data element.

DBMS　Database Management System.

Deviation　Defines the conditions and parameters for variance from the item/product design or process specifications, normally for a specific timeframe or specific number of units. Usually documented with a form. Should be posted in the document revision block.

DFT　Demand Flow Technology. See *JIT*.

Dispositioning　CM slang. Determining what to do with the old design parts resulting from a design change.

Doc/document　Usually refers to technical, product-related documents. Includes, but is not restricted to, design drawings and specifications. It is not media specific, and some documents may never take the "traditional" form of "formatted paper." Sometimes used as a reference to a change that affects only the document (doc or records change).

Document Management System　Allows users to store, search, and manipulate documents electronically and to maintain a library of text and images in a compact space. Many such systems also provide a means for passing documents across a network. See *PDM*, *PLM*.

Document representation　A set of digital files which, when viewed or printed together, collectively represent the entire document (for example, a set of raster files or a set of IGES files). Note: A document may have more than one document representation. Source: MIL Standard 2549.

DOD   Department Of Defense.

DOE   Department Of Energy.

ECN   Engineering Change Notice. Another generic term for an ECO. DOD term used when the organization writing the ECO does not have the master in its facility to accomplish the change and sends a version of the ECO (the ECN) to the owning facility to direct master update.

ECO   Engineering Change Order. Term used to refer to any form utilized to specifically define the change and to accomplish the evaluation/review, approval, planning and incorporation of the change. Other names frequently used for the same purpose – DCN, ECN, etc.

ECP   Engineering Change Proposal. Term used to refer to any form used to obtain customer review and/or approval of a change.

ECR   Engineering Change Request. Term used to refer to any form used to solicit the responsible engineer to take ownership of a problem or suggestion for possible change. (EAR – Engineering Action Request might be a better term because it gets the word "change" out of the process).

EDC   Engineering Document Control. A discipline similar to CM but focused on an organization's technical documents.

Effectivity   CM slang. A method of specifying when (usually a date) and at what point in the manufacturing process a design change will be made and/or which units have the change.

ERP   Enterprise Resources Planning. Software programs that are an extension of the manufacturing resources planning (MRP) concepts. These systems are used to take, make, ship and account for customer orders and thus to automate and integrate business, accounting and production management processes.

FCA   Functional Configuration Audit.

FCO   Field Change Order. A method or form for incorporation of a design change in units that have been shipped.

FDA   Food and Drug Administration.

Firmware   Computer programs, instructions or functions implemented in user-modifiable hardware. Such programs or instructions – stored permanently in programmable, read-only memories – may constitute a fundamental part of a hardware product.

Flow chart   Diagrammatic representation of the operations involved in a process or system. Flow lines and arrows indicate the sequence of operations and/or the flow of data or forms.

Flow diagram   Same as a flow chart with the party/department that performs the operation designated in the diagram.

Flow manufacturing   Other names: agile manufacturing; continuous (flow) manufacturing; demand-based conversion; JIT (just-in-time) manufacturing; lean manufacturing. A production technique in which the work moves from one operation to the next continuously (one piece at a time). Usually requires the rearrangement of the plant into lines and/or cells. Simplified scheduling and reporting appropriate for short production lead time. Demand-based flow links production schedules to customer demand for quick response and short lead time. Many of the advantages of mass production without long production runs; enabler for mass customization. Often incorporates just-in-time and Kanban techniques for material control.

GMP   Good Manufacturing Practices.

GT   Group Technology. The grouping of discrete items into families having similar design and/or manufacturing process characteristics. Source: *EIT Glossary*. See also **Part classification**.

I   Interchangeable. See course matter or F. Watts' book.

IE   Industrial Engineer.

Imaging   The electronic representation and storage of documents. Imaging systems typically allow retrieval and dissemination of those documents. Systems may be thought of as electronic vaults.

Interface   A shared boundary between two pieces of equipment or computer software code. The hardware and software needed to enable one device to communicate with another.

Item   A generic term for any part, component, assembly or product. Might also be used to refer to documents. Generally limited to things assigned part numbers.

JIT   Just In Time. An approach to manufacturing that stresses the benefits inherent in a "pull" system, wherein a small amount of material is brought to the workplace and put in a Kanban (location) only when it is needed. To achieve this goal each operation must be synchronized with those before and after it. Also called short-cycle manufacturing, demand flow technology, stockless production, zero inventories, etc. The primary goals are the reduction of inventory space and carrying costs.

JPEG   Joint Photographic Experts Group. A bitmap (raster) graphics format.

Kanban   Japanese terminology for one element for achieving JIT – the term specifically relating to the use of a location/card to indicate part status/quantity needs.

KISS   Keep It Swift and Simple (or Keep It Simple Stupid).

MC   Material Control.

MES   Manufacturing Execution Systems. Software to track work in process through detailed product routing and tracking, labor reporting, resource and rework management, production measurement and data collection. These systems are similar to MRP/ERP but generally used in process manufacturing (food, drug, beverage, etc.).

MRP   Material Requirements Planning. Later MRP II, Manufacturing Resources Planning.
Software programs that perform a variety of functions to aid in the manufacturing process. They use the bill of material, inventory data and the master production schedule to calculate requirements for materials and orders (MRP).
Software programs which do the above and include planning the use of company resources, suppliers, equipment and processes, and sometimes financial and distribution management (MRP II).
Subsequent improvements over time are termed ERP. May or may not interface with CAD, PLM or PDM systems.

NASA   National Aeronautics and Space Agency.

Network   Any system of computers and peripherals. Any combination of circuit elements in an electrical or hydraulic circuit.

NI   Non-Interchangeable.

NRA   Nuclear Regulatory Agency.

ODBC   Open Database Compliant. An approach to software/computing that stresses the interconnecting of systems based on compliance to established standards.

OODBMS   Object-Oriented Database Management System.

Parent/child   A descriptive term that represents the assembly and component relationship in the parts list or BOM.

Part   Any physical item without a parts list. Might also be called a piece part, material, item or component. A part/component to us could be an assembly or product to our supplier.

Part class or part classification   Methods to classify parts and documents of a product by their function or by the processes used to manufacture them. See also *GT*.

Part master/item master   Data/information related to the part or item regardless of where it is used.

PC   Personal Computer or Production Control.

PCB   Printed Circuit Board.

PDF   Portable Document Format. File format for distributing formatted documents, with fonts and graphics, in a read and print form that can be read by Adobe Systems Inc. Reader or similar programs. The user does not have to have the originating application.

PDM   Product Data Management. Software that helps manage design documents and data. May also be referred to as Product Information Management (PIM), Engineering Data Management (EDM), Engineering Information Management (EIM), or generically as file control or vaulting systems. See also *PLM*.

PDR   Preliminary Design Review.

PL   Parts List. A list of parts, subassemblies and sometimes reference documents for an assembly.

PLM   Product Lifecycle Management. Newer generation PDM.

PN   Part Number.

Process map   See *Block diagram*.

QA   Quality Assurance.

QC   Quality Control.

QE   Quality Engineering.

Records change   A term used to refer to a change, which affects only the document(s) and has no effect on the physical product. Sometimes referred to as a "doc" change or "doc only" change.

Release   The act of obtaining the required approvals to progress from one phase of design and manufacturing to the next phase.

Revision   A modification of any part of any product technical data or documents.

SCM   Supply Chain Management.

SCO   Software Change Order.

SN   Serial Number.

SPC Statistical Process Control. A quality control method focusing on continuous monitoring of the process rather than inspection of finished products, with the intent to achieve control of the process and eliminate defective product. Source: *Manufacturing Systems* glossary.

SQC Statistical Quality Control. Applies the laws of probability and statistical techniques to the observed characteristics of a product or process. Source: *Manufacturing Systems* glossary.

TE Test Engineer.

TIF/TIFF Tagged Image File Format. A bitmap (raster) graphics format.

TMI Too Much Information.

Vault Print/document storage, either electronic or physical. The PDM/PLM system's computerized data storage area and databases. Information stored in PDM/PLM vaults is controlled by system rules and processes. Source: *EIT Glossary.*

Version Non-interchangeable changes to an item or to software.

WIP Work In Process.

Workflow Any diagram depicting the flow of work. The software ability to graphically designate and change the distribution, routing for adding value and/or approval routing of documents related to a business process. Typically function or department specific.

Summary

If you have read or even just perused this work form cover to cover, you must be thoroughly overwhelmed by the sheer volume of potential measurements, metrics and reports. If a full-time person was added to your staff, it might still not be possible to produce all the metrics that you think are pertinent to your organization. It may be tempting to cast this book aside with a sigh and say something like: "That is nice, but who has time!"

So what can practically be done? Identify a process that you believe most needs improvement – perhaps the change process. Pick one phase of that process – perhaps the CM phase. Then:

- Assure that you understand and workflow diagram the current process
- Select the part(s) of that phase suspected to be in most trouble
- Identify a measurable "start" and "complete" for that portion of the process
- Use the "WIP count" method to estimate the thru-put time
- If the WIP method confirms your gut feeling, proceed to measure the time on every change
- Prepare a metric showing time, volume and WIP, for example.

The part of the process you choose might be "revision incorporation drafting," for example. On what date is the change sent to Design Drafting? On what date were all the masters updated and returned to the vault?

Measure that time on every change and summarize it at the end of each week. Make a metric plotting the time and add the volume and WIP. Include a note that indicates what you think the time should be – an interim goal. Share the results after a few weeks with key people and management.

If this is well received on the part of the key management, take on measurement of another portion of the process. Repeat the above steps for this portion – perhaps the effective date planning. Then the next, etc. until all of the CM change process is measured. Make a summary bar chart to display where the time-consumers are. Distribute that to key people and management noting which portions of the change process aren't yet measured.

Don't just point out where the problems exist. Include suggestions for process improvements. Try to get a key high-level manager excited about the lack of performance. Suggest a small improvement team be formed with that manager as the champion for the team. Suggest a person be added to or transferred to the CM function to do measurement and to relieve you of enough tasks to allow you to dedicate effort to the process improvement teamwork.

Lacking a management champion, do this yourself or with a key person or two. It can be fun and re-warding. If you become frustrated, move to a different process or part of a process. Always keep in mind:

- **Principle:** "It must be remembered that there is nothing more difficult to plan, more doubtful of success, nor more dangerous to manage than the creation of a new system … For the initiator has the enmity of all who would profit by the preservation of the old institutions and merely lukewarm defenders in those who would gain by the new ones."

(Machiavelli, 1513)

Good logic might suggest that continuous improvement is the practical path. Remember that creation of key metrics can shed light on a problem that will produce heat (recognition of the problem), which will likely produce a solution. Thus, the first steps toward improvement of a CM process are to document those processes and to measure them – to shed light on problems.

Index